A CLOSER WALK

Catherine Marshall

A CLOSER WALK

Edited by Leonard E. LeSourd

Published by
✓ chosen books

FLEMING H. REVELL COMPANY
OLD TAPPAN, NEW JERSEY

Scripture quotations are from:

The Amplified Bible © 1965 by the Zondervan Publishing House and The Lockman Foundation

The King James Version published by the American Bible Society, 1972

The Living Bible © 1971 by Tyndale House Publishers

The Bible, The James Moffatt Translation © 1954 by James A. R. Moffatt

The New English Bible, © 1970 by the Delegates of the Oxford University Press and the Syndics of the Cambridge University Press

The Holy Bible, New International Version, © 1978 by the International Bible Society, used by permission of Zondervan Bible Publishers

The New Testament in Modern English, J. B. Phillips, © 1972 by J. B. Phillips

The Holy Bible, Revised Standard Version, © 1946, 1952 by Division of Christian Education of the National Council of the Churches of Christ in the United States of America

Good News Bible, The Bible in Today's English Version, © 1976 by the American Bible Society

We are grateful for use of the lyrics on pages 7, 174, and 178, © Singspiration of the Zondervan Corporation.

Over the years, Catherine Marshall shared many of the insights from her journals with the readers of *Guideposts* magazine. These articles are copyright by Guideposts Associates, Inc. Copyright © 1964, 1965, 1967, 1968, 1969, 1970, 1976, 1977, 1979, 1983 by Guideposts Associates, Inc., Carmel, New York 10512.

Library of Congress Cataloging in Publication Data

Marshall, Catherine, 1914–
  A closer walk.

  1. Christian life—1960– . 2. Marshall,
Catherine, 1914– . I. LeSourd, Leonard.
II. Title.
BV4501.2.M3642 1986   248.4   86-10045
ISBN 0-8007-9065-0

I am weak but Thou art strong
Jesus, keep me from all wrong;
I'll be satisfied as long
As I walk, dear Lord, close to Thee.

Just a closer walk with Thee
Grant it, Jesus, if You please;
Daily walking close to Thee
Let it be, dear Lord, let it be.

Acknowledgments _____

Special thanks go to Jeanne Sevigny, Catherine's trusted secretary and close friend of fourteen years, who not only did the typing of Catherine's handwritten journal items, but served as advisor on the selection of material used in this book. Also to Regina Trollinger and Yvonne Burgan for their secretarial skills.

A big debt of gratitude to Elizabeth Sherrill, whose book expertise guided Catherine for twenty-two years through the writing of *Beyond Our Selves, Christy, Adventures in Prayer, Something More, Meeting God At Every Turn,* and *Julie,* and who edited the editor of this manuscript with her usual sensitivity and brilliance.

Contents

Section Two—Adventuresome Living

Section Three—Christian Growth

Section Four—His Strength in Our Weakness

Section Five—Spiritual Warfare

Section Six—The Final Victory

Using This Book . . .
On Your Own Walk ＿＿＿＿＿

For you—as it has for me—*A Closer Walk* can become not so much a book as a traveling companion, inviting us to share the rough places and the mountain tops with a fellow pilgrim, Catherine Marshall.

In personal journals kept during her most creative years as a writer, wife, and mother, Catherine recorded her encounters with such roadblocks as . . .

> Criticalness
> The Poverty Complex
> Resentment
> The Dry Period
> Chronic Worry
> Illness

Most importantly, she described also the "way through," which she found in the Scriptures.

Throughout her journey, the Bible was the traveler's staff on which Catherine leaned. From every page shines her commitment to daily Bible reading—and her faithfulness in applying what she read to that day's need.

If you're like me, two things will happen as you make this pilgrimage with Catherine. Your own Bible reading will become more focused, more personal, infinitely more exciting. And you will be nudged to start your own "travel diary."

This was exactly the impact on Len LeSourd, after reading the first of these entries. Before he married Catherine, Len recalls today, he had never thought of putting his own spiritual struggles down on paper— certainly not *as* he was living through them.

Shortly after their marriage in 1959, however, a moving van delivered Catherine's possessions to their first home. Len watched in husbandly amusement as Catherine hovered over one particular carton, clearly attaching more value to it than to the clothes, dishes, and pieces of furniture that arrived along with it.

"My journals," Catherine explained.

When Len still looked blank, she drew from the box a dark green volume, four inches by seven, with "Year Book 1934" stamped on the front. Catherine had filled the book with reactions to campus life that sophomore year at Agnes Scott College in Georgia. Three more green journals in the box covered the years through 1937.

There was a five-year diary for 1938–42, recording Catherine's soul-searching as she met and eventually married Peter Marshall. Journals of various shapes and colors detailed her years as Peter's wife: the birth of their son, her own serious illness, the loss of her young husband. As a widow in the 1950s, Catherine entered her spiritual questing in a succession of spiral-bound notebooks.

In growing astonishment, Len helped Catherine store the volumes on a shelf. What discipline and devotion these thousands of pages represented! Where would a person find the time?

Len soon found out. Early in the morning, Catherine would take from a dresser drawer a bright red hardcover *Daily Reminder*. No amount of fatigue from the previous day spent coralling three small stepchildren, no pleas from a sleepy husband, could keep her from this daily appointment-in-writing with God.

When Catherine finally allowed Len to read some current entries, he understood her commitment to the discipline. These were more than simply prayer records, more even than the joyful recording of answers. The act of writing itself was part of Catherine's relationship with God; it helped define her needs, focus her prayers, act out her trust.

Len soon joined her in this early morning time and began keeping a prayer record of his own. His approach was somewhat different from Catherine's. Each individual's format, style, and frequency will of course be unique. But right from the start Len discovered the secret that Catherine had known for years: *putting prayer issues on paper* eliminates the vagueness that so often diffuses personal devotions.

Her lively new family, Len confesses, sometimes made it difficult for Catherine to keep a set time of day for her journal. Before long she was making her entries at any and every moment when the dust settled.

But make them she did. For the next twenty-three years Catherine poured her hopes and dreams, questions asked of God and answers received from Him, into the growing collection of *Daily Reminders*. The current volume accompanied the LeSourds on trips, appeared in the laundry room and at the breakfast table. When Catherine's pen was stilled on March 18, 1983, these journals were her rich legacy to Len, with instructions to disclose the contents with wisdom and discretion.

A Closer Walk is the result.

It will remain only "someone else's story," however, unless you and I come along.

Elizabeth Sherrill

A CLOSER WALK

A Woman Called Catherine ____

The first time I saw Catherine was on December 1, 1955, at a luncheon in the Waldorf Astoria ballroom, where she was to receive the Salvation Army's 1955 Award for her contributions to "the spiritual life of her time." A poll that year had listed her as one of the ten most admired women in America. As the dignitaries, mostly men, filed onto the stage, Catherine, overshadowed by their physical presence, looked small, fragile, a bit overwhelmed.

I stared at her more closely. What was the secret of her sudden propulsion onto the national stage? Writing a best-selling religious book like *A Man Called Peter* couldn't do it alone. Watching her animated gestures as she conversed with master of ceremonies Walter Hoving (president of prestigious Tiffany's), noting her trim figure and stylish grooming, I decided that she was a phenomenon—a devout preacher's wife who had also won the admiration of nonbelievers.

How had she done it?

I listened carefully to Catherine's speech that described the "supernatural intervention of God" at Dunkirk during World War II. *Unlikely subject for a sophisticated New York City gathering,* I thought to myself. But she avoided religious clichés and held her audience. *A high voltage, spiritual woman, but with worldly wisdom,* I concluded.

Some months later Catherine was invited to speak at our Young Adult Group at the Marble Collegiate Church. There, I met her face to face for the first time, bathed for a short moment in her warm smile and controlled intensity. Yet, too, a shyness. In her speech I liked the practical way she applied biblical truths to her personal struggles.

As the editor of *Guideposts,* I wrote and asked her if she would write a piece for our small inspirational magazine, which had just reached a circulation of one hundred thousand. We talked over the phone about it. Her article "How You Can Receive God's Guidance" sparked eager reader response.

In 1957 I was functioning in the role of single parent, trying to rear three small children in Carmel, New York, while commuting over a hundred miles each day to work in New York City. It was a lonely, difficult time for me. One night I poured out my agony to God and laid before Him my need for a wife. Then, remembering Catherine's article on guidance, I took out a yellow pad, prepared to write down the names of any possible mates He might suggest.

Catherine's name popped into my mind.

It seemed almost ludicrous to tie Catherine Marshall to my plea for a partner. "That can't be your idea, Lord," I said, dismissing the thought.

Then I recalled Catherine's book *To Live Again* and the chapter that had entranced me—"They Walk in Wistfulness." In it she had given a poignant answer to a doctor's question about her emotional well-being. I reread the chapter and came to these words:

Do you really want to know what it feels like to be a widow? God made men and women for each other. Any other way of life is wrong; because it is abnormal. The last few months it's been like having a gnawing hunger, a haunting wistfulness at the center of life. I can forget about it for short periods—ignore it sometimes. But it's always there—always—and I'm afraid not even you can prescribe any pills that can cure it.

Elsewhere in that same chapter she wrote:

The need is to love and to be loved—that ultimate of life. Could I, and all those like me who walk the earth in wistfulness, find the way to trust God even for that?

Suddenly I knew that Catherine and I had something in common—loneliness. But so little else, it seemed. The whole idea was ridiculous. I ticked off the reasons why.

First and foremost, who would want to follow the Peter and Catherine act? Their romance and marriage had entranced and stirred millions of people through her best-selling book; more millions had been captivated by the beautifully-done movie of *A Man Called Peter*.

Why would I want to marry a super-spiritual Christian celebrity? Who was almost five years older than I was?

Even more to the point, why would Catherine, at age forty-four, even supposing she should be attracted to me as an individual, want to marry a man who was rearing three small children?

Looked at logically, the idea of Catherine and me pairing up made little sense from any standpoint.

But . . . a voice deep inside reminded me, God is not bound by logic.

The least I could do was give it one good shot, I decided. If God was in it, I'd soon know. So I called Catherine, said *Guideposts* was looking for another article (true), and asked her if I could come to Washington and take her out for dinner. Requesting a dinner date should signal to her that I had more in mind than just an article.

She parried that proposal with the suggestion we make it lunch.
Strike one.

I took a plane from New York to Washington, rented a car, and drove to her town house just off Wisconsin Avenue. Catherine emerged, wearing a dark blue dress with white collar and cuffs; silver earrings and a diamond brooch added distinct feminine touches. A lovely woman. Something quickened inside me.

Lunch at a Georgetown restaurant, however, was a letdown. Catherine was friendly and full of ideas for an article. Yet she neatly sidestepped all probing into her personal life. She was the consummate professional.

Strike two.

I drove her back to her town house, prepared to say goodbye and dismiss once and for all any thoughts of a personal relationship. Just before opening the car door, I happened to ask her a question regarding the Holy Spirit. It was as if I had found the combination to a valuable safe. An excited conversation followed that lasted for another half hour. Our two spirits had touched, then been ignited.

I was still at bat.

A week or so later I wrote to Catherine, asking if I could see her on the way back from an upcoming trip to California. With my plans a bit uncertain, I listed two possible dates, told her I would telephone beforehand. There wasn't time before I left for the coast for her to reply.

I did call Catherine from California—several times—but got no answer. The morning I was to fly from Los Angeles to Washington I called again—still nobody there. Then I came to a conclusion.

This is ridiculous. Catherine has no interest in me personally. I'm being silly to pursue this. Besides, she's not even home.

I changed my reservation from Washington to New York, flew home, and decided to forget the inner nudging that I should seek a romance with Catherine.

Strike three?

No, not quite. A foul tip, perhaps, that the catcher dropped. Several days later I received a letter from Catherine. "What happened to you?" she wrote. "You asked me to hold two dates. I did, but you never appeared. Or called. Is anything wrong?"

I was startled. Then stimulated. Catherine was obviously annoyed with me. But that was not all bad. In fact, it was many moons better than indifference.

In a spirit of contrition, I started to call Catherine, then stopped. A new, more direct approach was needed. *Drop your editorial front, Len; don't be defensive. Approach her man to woman.* In this vein, I wrote her a letter.

In *Meeting God At Every Turn* Catherine describes how she reacted to this change of style in me:

> There was nothing of the professional editor about the letter I received from Len several days later. "I would like to know you better," he wrote. "How do you react to this idea? We'll choose a day, and then you write on your calendar three letters: F U N. I'll pick you up in the morning in my car and we'll just take off to the beach or the mountains or whatever."
>
> The letter seemed deliberately couched to say, "If you're interested in pursuing this relationship, let's have a go at it. If not, then tell me so right now."
>
> I liked the approach. We set a day in early August. Len telephoned the night before from a Washington motel to say that he would call for me at 10:30 the next morning. He was delighted when I suggested fixing a picnic lunch.
>
> The next morning turned out to be a beautiful summer day, not too hot. When I met Len at my front door, I found myself slipping easily into the adventurous mood he had suggested. He put the picnic basket in the trunk of his car and we climbed into the front seat. "What do you prefer," he asked casually, "ocean or mountains?"
>
> "I would choose the mountains," I replied.
>
> "Which direction?"
>
> I aimed him west toward Skyline Drive. As we drove along, I studied this fortyish editor sitting beside me. He was of medium height; dark hair beginning to gray; lithe, athletic figure. His gray-blue eyes were direct, warm, the lids often crinkling with humor.

He was a good conversationalist, probing but relaxed. I relaxed, too.

It was going to be a good day.

It was a good day, an amazing day. We talked for almost eleven hours straight. All my resistance to following the Peter Marshall romance, to her "super spirituality" and to our age difference dissolved in my astonishment over Catherine's physical warmth, simplicity, and earthy good humor. I was overwhelmed by the idea that God had perceived all this beforehand and had brought us together. During that one astounding day I fell in love with Catherine and began to think ahead toward marriage.

Catherine was slower in coming to this conclusion. She had to face more obstacles than I did. Mine had been mostly ego problems. Hers were substantive: taking on three small children, turning at a right angle to the life that had seemed to stretch so comfortably and predictably ahead of her—for which her dream house was even then being built. This home in Bethesda, Maryland, was to be ready for occupancy within a few months; Catherine had personally designed it to meet her career-woman needs.

That she was able to overcome these obstacles had to be the Lord's doing. For weeks she prayed, probed the Scriptures. And it was during this time of her intense searching that I began to find answers to the question I asked myself at that Salvation Army luncheon: What was the special charisma in this woman that had captured both believers and nonbelievers?

First, a down-to-earth quality that shunned subterfuge and embraced candor and openness. Ever since the success of *A Man Called Peter,* people had tried to put her on a spiritual pedestal. She resisted, refused to play the role of guru, insisted that she was a struggler for truth like everyone else.

Second, the spirit of adventure. She saw her faith in this light. Jesus was bold, imaginative, unpredictable. God's plan for each life was unique, did not fit any set formula. Both the death of her first husband and the rebirth of love interest in her life were totally unexpected, yet within the illimitable providence of the God she knew.

Third, vulnerability. Catherine was honest about her flaws, admitting her inadequacies in such areas as child rearing and certain social situations. Result: she learned from her mistakes. This quality also made her open to editorial advice in every book she wrote but one, and that one had to be abandoned.

I learned a lot about Catherine during this period, but the deeper secret of her success eluded me. That first date, rambling along the Skyline Drive, was in early August; we were married three months later on November 14, 1959.

Catherine had huge adjustments to make. She sold her Washington dream house to move to Chappaqua, forty miles north of New York City, so that I could continue to commute to my job at *Guideposts* in the city. My children—Linda, ten; Chester, six; Jeffrey, three—had been through a deeply unsettling two years, adjusting to a variety of housekeepers. They had mixed feelings toward moving into a new house, and especially toward "the new Mommie that Daddy's bringing home."

Catherine's son, Peter John, nineteen, was going through a period of rebellion at Yale. It's hard enough for a young person to cope with one celebrity parent, but Peter's father and mother both were "Christian personages." Peter told us one day with a straight face that when he graduated he wanted to be a beach boy at Virginia Beach.

Catherine and I had so many things to pray about that we began to rise an hour early each morning to read the Bible and seek answers together. Her current journal lay open beside us in these pre-dawn prayer times, recording our changing needs, His unchanging faithfulness.

Our togetherness as an author-editor team was tested early in our marriage. Catherine had already been working over a year researching her novel *Christy* and had written some fifty or so pages. One day she handed me her manuscript. Outside of her typist, I would be the first to read it. I started in with much anticipation.

Two hours later I faced a dilemma. The manuscript was wordy, short on action—yes, a bit dull. Conversation between mountain people was almost undecipherable because of Catherine's attempt to spell out the dialect as she had heard it. On the plus side, the characters were truly believable. Should I tell her the whole truth, or just center on the good things I saw in the manuscript?

Drawing a deep breath, I told her the truth as I saw it. She flinched for a moment, then stared at me with a new light in her eyes. "You're right on all counts," she admitted. "I felt it was weak, but hoped somehow I was too close to it to see its strengths." She sighed, "Let's start with the mountain dialect."

Thus did I pass the first crucial test of our professional relationship. If I had been less than honest, she would have eventually gotten the needed critique from Ed Kuhn, her McGraw-Hill editor. But she and I were full collaborators at work, now, as well as in the home.

As the years passed Catherine and I, as a writer-editor team, became more and more productive: between us we were responsible for nearly one hundred *Guideposts* articles and more than thirty published books. There were dozens of appearances as a speaking team; numerous courses conducted together on Christian subjects, highlighting the movement of the Holy Spirit.

I have one major regret about all this. We didn't take enough time to smell the flowers, to learn what it really means to take a vacation. We went from deadline to deadline, from crisis to crisis, dealing with what had to be done, forgetting too often to mark on our calendar those letters F U N. I feel deeply convicted about this, but the truth is that Catherine and I were workaholics.

During our twenty-three years of marriage I did discover the secrets behind her extraordinary gifts of communication. There were two. One came out through the dedication she showed in rearing my three young children—despite lungs that never operated at more than seventy-five percent normal capacity. It emerged as she struggled for the precise descriptive phrase in her writing, as she sought the exactly right color for a living room chair, in her search for tonal perfection in stereo music. She tried to lift the sights of her family and friends by planting dreams in our hearts of achievements that appeared beyond us.

This reach toward excellence was a part of everything she did.

One example, I'll never forget. Catherine was preparing a dinner party for special friends. The day before, she asked me to drive her to Falls Church just outside of Washington—an hour's trip. "Some errands," she told me.

One errand, as it turned out. At a bakery, which sold a certain kind of macaroons. As we drove about Falls Church looking for this bakery in steamy weather, I fought off a growing irritation.

"Catherine, why are these macaroons so important to you?"

"I have a great recipe for grinding them into a wonderful sauce."

"A sauce! For what?"

"For the fruit compote I'm planning for dessert."

I turned and looked at her in amazement. "We're taking three hours out of a day, in terrible heat, to drive through miserable traffic to buy a bag of macaroons so people can pour a little sauce on their dessert!"

"That's right," she said. "It's the sauce that makes the dessert."

That was Catherine. She gave herself unreservedly to what she was doing, would settle for nothing but one hundred percent, was one-eyed in the scriptural sense whether it was writing, speaking, painting, decorating, preparing meals, building family life.

Her intensity spilled over into everything and I loved to watch it erupt. One night during the late 1960s, she strode into our bedroom where I was reading and began to pace the floor, face furious. "What's happened?" I asked in alarm.

She didn't answer right away, just stared at me with tears in her eyes. "I'm so upset I can hardly speak," she said.

"Over what?"

"Viet Nam! We shouldn't be fighting there. It's wrong . . . wrong . . . wrong. God will punish us for this."

I looked at her in amazement, surprised again at the emotion she poured into her convictions that could focus one moment on a child's poor study habits, the next on a war ten thousand miles away.

But there's another more profound reason for Catherine's extraordinary accomplishments. Her love of Jesus, expressed through a love affair with Scripture.

Bibles were scattered throughout our house . . . all editions, plus reference books and concordances. We often went to bed, turned out the light, and listened to a chapter of Scripture on tape. If she could have found a way to spread Bible passages on a slice of bread, Catherine would have devoured it.

When upset or under spiritual assault or in physical pain, Catherine would go to her office, kneel by her chair, and open her Bible to the fifty-third chapter of Isaiah, or the ninety-first Psalm, or the second chapter of Acts, or the eighth chapter of Romans. She would read, then pray, then read, then pray some more. She liked to pray with the Bible clutched in her hands; it gave her strength. She would rest her case on its promises. Catherine didn't read the Bible for solace or inspiration, but to have an encounter with the Lord. Sometimes she emerged from these sessions contrite, sometimes at peace, sometimes still in turmoil. I think these were the most intense moments of her life.

All of Catherine's Bibles are marked with underlinings; color shadings make certain passages almost leap out at you. Question marks and exclamation points dot page after page. A long comment will be scribbled at the top or bottom or along the side. Sometimes "Yes! Yes! Yes!" indicates Catherine's exuberant confirmation of a teaching.

Some of her happiest moments were when she was preparing a Bible study for one of our classes or for a writing project. She chose our king-size bed for this adventure, propping herself up with pillows, while Bibles, reference books, a thesaurus, a concordance, and yellow pads were spread all about her.

Catherine's passion for the Word permeated her whole life. It undergirded her writing. It formed a base for us as a married team in the making of family decisions. It provided substance to her counseling of people through the mail. I'm convinced it was also the basis for her inner vitality, her charisma, and the mantle of authority she wore with some reluctance.

Her grappling with the Word mostly took place in the early morning hours, as she fed her questions and discoveries into her journals. Material from these writings—her "closer walk" with her Lord—provide the content for this book. They cover our struggles in bringing together two broken homes, learning to relate to children and stepchildren—and later, our relationship to their spouses and our grandchildren.

What shines through Catherine's words is that Christian growth and adventuring never stop. The search for more of the truth is endlessly absorbing: the promises God holds out are worth every moment of struggle, the "walk" never arrives at some static, fixed point, but leads on into ever deeper intimacy with God.

A Closer Walk is the record of Catherine's encounters with the Lord of Scripture along the way, most appearing in print for the first time. The book is divided into six sections that move chronologically from our early life together as a family, through Christian creativity and growth, into spiritual warfare, to the final triumph of her death.

Years before Catherine died, we had talked about the probability that I would outlive her. Since I had worked so closely with her on every writing project, she knew we were in accord on one basic principle—no book of her writings would see print unless it measured up to her standard of excellence. The principal guardians of this standard were to be myself and her long-time friend and editorial advisor, Elizabeth Sherrill, whose talents we both admire so much and who has carefully gone over this manuscript.

May this book bless you who read it, and stimulate you to seek "a closer walk" with Jesus.

Leonard E. LeSourd

Section One

The Home
As His Classroom

U*pon returning from our honeymoon in late 1959, Catherine and I confronted all the problems and adjustments involved in bringing together two broken homes. Catherine's greatest self-doubt centered around the responsibility for mothering three young stepchildren. (Her son, Peter John Marshall, was attending college.) Always a perfectionist, she felt she lacked the patient, accepting qualities of an ideal mother.*

The early morning time when we sought answers together in the Bible became lifeblood for Catherine. Time and again from Scripture she drew insight and answers. Praying together in advance of the inevitable conflicts and confrontations solidified our marriage. It is hard to stay upset or angry at your mate when you are sitting up in bed side by side, holding hands, reading God's Word.

The setting for the following episodes was an eight-room home in Chappaqua, New York, a suburban community some forty miles north of New York City, where we lived for the first five years of our marriage.

LL

I

*A New Way
to See Jesus*

*A*s Len and I begin our new life together, I'm enjoying a new way to read the New Testament—undoubtedly a way known to many Christians through the centuries but new to me: during my early morning devotions I'm reading the words as if Jesus were speaking directly to me.

At the time of my discovery, I was going through the Gospels consecutively, desiring above all else to get a vivid portrait of Jesus. And a portrait emerged all right, not so much what He looked like, as the characteristics of His person. I discovered in Him one who is totally alive—physically stalwart, emotionally sensitive. Humor, I definitely found. And grief—not for Himself, but for others' hurts and the tragic havoc that sin brings. And love, an amazing love that pours out of Him with never any effort to hide it or dam it up. Yet it is a love with steel in it.

Over and over I have come upon this steel—a note of stringency in Jesus' conversation and His way of dealing with people that, for the most part, seems alien to the teaching in our churches today. Never have I found a trace of coddling or compromising or self-protectiveness in Him.

For example, there was the Pharisee who asked Jesus to lunch at his house. Jesus accepted. But if there was anything pleasant about the conversation around the table, we were not told so in Luke's account. Indeed, centuries later, the words all but blister the page:

> But woe to you Pharisees! for you tithe mint and rue and every herb,
> and neglect justice and the love of God . . . you love the best seat
> in the synagogues and salutations in the market places . . . you are
> like graves which are not seen, and men walk over them without
> knowing it.
>
> Luke 11:42–44 RSV

It is clear that Christ chose to tell this particular man and his guests the simple, straightforward truth rather than keeping quiet or being socially correct. That takes courage of a rare sort, and Jesus must have known full well that it could lead only to a cross.

There is an unexpected dividend from reading the New Testament as if Jesus were speaking to me: when I look away from the problems in my new marriage to turn my full attention to Jesus, He proves Himself alive by concerning Himself with my life, family, and friends and talking to me about these matters morning after morning.

Last week, for example, as I read the twelfth chapter of Luke, it was as though Jesus were saying:

> Beware of pretending before the family to be something you are not,
> or to have attained spiritual values that you have not attained. This

is hypocrisy. And nothing is more futile than trying to keep anything secret. There is nothing covered up among family members that is not going to be uncovered.

Later in the same chapter He seemed to tell me:

You think that because members of your family believe in Me, all should be peaceful and serene. Not so. My presence is not going to bring sweet peace and an easy time. On occasions, My thoughts and My way will bring severe discord. Do not be surprised when this happens. Realize that out of temporary disharmony—if it includes honest facing-up—comes growth for each member of the family and a further knitting together in Me.

This new way of letting Jesus speak to me may help me relate to a new neighbor too. She's asked me to assist in a community project in which I do not believe. I was puzzled as to how to handle the situation without hurting her feelings. In the eleventh chapter of Luke I heard:

You think that you do not want to tell your neighbor the truth because you do not want to hurt her. The real reason is that you want to protect yourself from her displeasure, or antagonism. It is wrong to keep quiet because you care more about her friendship (or anyone else's) than you care about her growth in Me. That is just another way of putting yourself first.

What are the results of these meditations? Increased honesty in our family has already led to more openness toward God in the lives of two of our children. I find that I'm less threatened by family arguments. So far I have not found the way or the courage to be honest with my friend. I ducked out of the project through an excuse.

But this I can say—the resurrected Jesus is a continual reality in my life. How can I ever find words to express the joy of His presence?

2

Stepmothering

*T*his morning I am pondering my bizarre dream of last night to see
if the Lord is telling me something through it:

In my dream a small animal emerged from a swelling near my
shoulder. Looking more closely, I saw that the animal was wounded.
"Those cuts will have to be sewn up," I thought, and then I woke up.

As I listened for God's word about the dream, I recalled how both
Len and I have referred to the two small boys as being like bear cubs
the way they roll and romp about the family room. Yesterday they
broke a vase doing this. I have to admit that sometimes the children
"get under my skin." Obviously the Lord is pointing out that changes
need to be made in my attitude.

Part of what Len and I have to resolve comes down to the proper order he places on his new wife and his children by a previous marriage. All the stepmother tales in fairy stories and folklore tell us that we are confronting something basic and difficult here.

Len's emotions toward his flesh and blood are *so* strong that perhaps it is against nature for him to try to put his wife first. In his mind, he's done this, but his instinctive emotion is to defend and protect his children. Yet not to put the wife first is to risk disaster in the marriage.

I turned to the nineteenth chapter of Matthew:

> For this reason a man shall leave his father and mother and be joined
> to his wife, and the two shall become one.
>
> Matthew 19:5 RSV

Fortunately, Len and I can pray together and can talk over these problems. I was able to tell him about my dream without fearing he would use it against me. We are learning to admit our weaknesses to each other.

3

Around the
Dinner Table

After much experimentation, Len and I have settled on the evening meal as the ideal time and place for growing as a family. Mornings are too pressured, evenings too filled with school work, meetings, phone calls.

Being at the dinner table each night of the week is a command performance for Len and myself, Linda, Chester, and Jeff. No TV dinners in front of the tube. No dinners for our children at friends' houses except on weekends. A major effort by Len and me to keep our professional activities from interfering with this time.

The meal begins with grace, and the children do most of the

praying, learning to overcome shyness until they can talk to God easily. Soon I hope we'll learn to say grace just as naturally when we eat as a family in restaurants.

Len and I try not to dominate the ensuing conversation, but draw out each child. "What did you learn today in school, Chester? . . . Which teacher do you like the most, Linda? . . . Who is your best friend, Jeff?"

Criticism in this setting, we learned, quenches fragile spirits; it's better saved for one-on-one encounters. After dinner there's a reading from Scripture and family prayer around the table. One of our main objectives is to show Jesus as so engaging a Person that we would all enjoy it if He joined us at the table.

"Jesus had a sense of humor," I mentioned once.

This seemed to surprise the children so the next night I came to the table armed with examples from Scripture. About the hypocrisy of the Pharisees He said, "You blind guides, straining out a gnat and swallowing a camel" (Matthew 23:24 RSV).

This is the humor of exaggeration, I explained, pointing out that Jesus' humor was always for a purpose. Sometimes it was His bridge to an individual He would otherwise have had trouble reaching. Most often it was to illuminate a truth.

There was the occasion when Christ joshed His disciples about spiritual timidity: "Is a lamp brought in to be put under a bushel, or under a bed?" (Mark 4:21 RSV). The point He was making: "I need disciples who don't hide their light."

When the apostles became too impressed with the crowds Jesus was drawing, knowing full well that crowds gather for many reasons, Jesus commented dryly, "Wherever the carcass lies, there will the vultures gather" (Matthew 24:28 MOFFATT).

Once we reread the Gospels, watching for Christ's wit, we find it everywhere. "Can one blind man be guide to another blind man? Surely they will both fall into the ditch" (Luke 6:39 PHILLIPS). Or the comment made about the rich man who valued his possessions too much. "It is easier for a camel to go through the eye of a needle than for a rich man to enter the kingdom of God" (Luke 18:25 NEB).

To awaken people at every level of their being, Jesus used every weapon of language and communication to achieve His goals; most effective were the humorous thrust and banter about those who put on airs and think more highly of themselves than they should. Jesus sees all our incongruities and absurdities, and He laughs along with us.

As the result of these dinner table discussions, we're all finding that our spontaneity and fervor in worshiping Him increase. Our goal with the children: to help them see in Christ an incredible Man with that rare blend found nowhere else—purity, strength, compassion, and sparkling humor.

4
Loving the Unlovely

As I look out over the bright greenery of our backyard this morning, I realize how hard it is for me to love people, even members of my own family, when I disapprove of their behavior. I know this is wrong, Lord Jesus, because You demonstrated time after time that it is possible, even necessary, to love people without judgment.

There was the woman taken in adultery and about to be stoned when You asked the mob surrounding her, "If any one of you is without sin, let him be the first to throw a stone at her." As You told her to go and sin no more, I could almost hear the caring quality of Your voice. Likewise with the woman You met at the well, the one who had had five husbands. Uncondemning love was in Your manner.

I have no trouble forgiving certain people, but recently I have seen that the forgiveness is not complete in Your eyes until I can love them too.

Ever since we moved here to Chappaqua, Marilyn[1] has been a thorn in my side. She's overbearing, overweight, and always overreacting. Her criticalness rubs me raw. Forgive her, sure. Love her, so hard for me. We can't manufacture love, can we? Until now I haven't even been willing for *You* to love Marilyn *through* me.

Queer about love . . . Is it a quality so of a piece that when we deliberately withhold it from any single human being, we deny love itself and, in the end, are rendered incapable of loving?

So last night, down on my knees in Len's presence, I confessed all this. With Len and You as witnesses, I'm giving You permission to give me the gift of love for Marilyn.

But this morning I'm not willing to stop there; I would like to be able to love people the way You love them. In Your Word this morning I came across some verses that give me a handle on how.

In 2 Peter 1, the apostle rejoices in the "precious and very great promises" by which we may be "partakers of the divine nature." Then he gives us a ladder of seven steps leading to this high goal:

1) To faith, add *virtue*. (v. 5)
2) To virtue, add *knowledge*. (v. 5)
3) To knowledge, add *self-control*. (v. 6)
4) To self-control, add *steadfastness*. (v. 6)
5) To steadfastness, add *godliness*. (v. 6)
6) To godliness, add *brotherly affection*. (v. 7)
7) To brotherly affection will then be added, *love*. (v. 7)

"For if these things are yours and abound," Peter concludes, "they keep you from being ineffective or unfruitful in the knowledge of our Lord Jesus Christ" (v. 8, RSV).

I want to climb that ladder, Lord, to be able to know You and love You more than ever before.

---

[1] Not her real name.

5

Seeking Excellence

I've been troubled about Linda's school work. Considering her high IQ she's not doing anything like her best. Last night at the dinner table I told her about one of my favorite Bible verses, which appears no less than three times in the Old Testament: He maketh my feet like hinds' feet, and setteth me upon my high places (Psalm 18:32–33, 2 Samuel 22:33-34, and Habakkuk 3:19 KJV).

"What in the world does that mean?" she asked, with a frown on her freckled face.

To answer, I told her about a friend of mine. . . .

When I was six years old, this family friend whom we called "Auntie Chamberlain" purchased the book *Hiawatha* for me. But this was no ordinary copy. It had hand-cut paper, beautiful illustrations, a pronouncing vocabulary for difficult Indian names, even a section for handicraft projects.

She had searched all over town to find it. And this was so typical of Auntie Chamberlain—a woman who gave herself totally to life. Auntie Chamberlain taught me the importance of doing every task with my whole heart. Soon I discovered that family games—like Parcheesi— were the most fun when played with total enthusiasm and concentration. Piano lessons took on added luster when I not only learned to read a piece of music, but also memorized it. School assignments were more fun when I did more than the minimum required.

I found that something more important than good grades came from this approach: a deep inner satisfaction, a glow, a happiness. And conversely, I discovered that when I undertook any project halfheartedly, the result was usually half successful.

Later on, while living in Washington, I saw to my delight this "Auntie Chamberlain quality" in another individual—Dr. Lida Earhart. She, too, gave all of herself to whatever task she undertook and had been the first woman to attain the rank of full professor at Columbia University. After retiring, she came to Washington to live and regularly attended services at our New York Avenue Presbyterian Church.

One day someone asked Miss Earhart to give a talk on the Book of Job at the monthly meeting of the church women's association. This was probably a tossed-off invitation, with the usual kind of talk expected. But the talk turned out to be far from usual. For two months Miss Earhart had studied the Book of Job. She had researched the archeological features of the time of Job and his contemporaries. She had read biblical scholars' analyses of the book. She had pondered deeply the book's theme: the problem of evil in our world. The result was one of the most memorable presentations I ever have heard.

Even more remarkable, she had done all that work for an ordinary church meeting. Nothing extraordinary had been asked or expected. Yet she knew *the secret of hinds' feet.*

"What is the secret?" Linda asked.

"The rear feet of the female red deer, known also as the *hind,*" I said, "step in precisely the same spot where the front feet have just been. Every motion of the hind is followed through with this same single-focused consistency, making it the most sure-footed of all mountain animals."

As the feet of the female deer are to the mountains, I told her, so is the mind of man to the heights of life. "Ask yourself—how many things have I done with single-minded devotion, nothing held back?"

"Not many," she admitted.

"It's not easy in our modern world," I agreed, "to make our lives like hinds' feet. Too much today is done with minimal effort. This attitude can begin with school work done sloppily—but there's no joy in halfhearted efforts."

Linda listened with real interest to this biblical simile. Lord, make it come alive in her life!

6

The Contagion of Joy

As I absorb the Gospels this September morning, I'm seeing Jesus so clearly as a vital young Man who loved life and was filled with joy.

I'm influenced no doubt by my experience last month [August 1961] at a conference of The Fellowship of Christian Athletes in Estes Park, Colorado, where I spoke to the wives of the coaches and leaders. I never had seen so much muscle and maleness packed into one area. During the entire week there was a virile, vibrant atmosphere. And who was the central figure? Jesus Christ!

Of primary interest to me was the involvement of my son Peter, who had graduated from Yale the previous June. Peter admitted his purpose in coming to the conference was to get close to nationally known athletes. "I'm not interested in hearing any Sunday school stories," he told Len and me. During high school and college to my great dismay he had rejected his Christian heritage.

Instead of Sunday school stories, Peter heard some of the biggest names in sports unashamedly tell how they had found joy in the Christian faith. From the beginning my son was swept along in the excitement of young men singing, shouting, laughing, competing, and praying together. By the fourth day he was literally catapulted into making a personal commitment of his life to Jesus Christ as Savior and Lord.

"It is an awesome thing when you meet Jesus for the first time," he told me later. Gone was his bored, know-it-all attitude, in its place a new aliveness. A decision to enter Princeton Theological Seminary followed a few weeks later.

It makes me eager to take a fresh look at the qualities of the One who has such an attraction for young people—in His time and ours. The Gospel picture of Him is of a joyous man with a buoyant zest for life. The New Testament in one place describes Him as "anointed . . . with the oil of gladness" (Hebrews 1:9 KJV).

As I read through the Gospels, I see that Jesus had quite a bit to say about joy. We are *not* invited to a relationship that will take away our fun but asked to "enter into the joy of [our] Lord" (Matthew 25:21 KJV). The purpose of His coming to earth, Jesus said, was in order that our *joy might be full!* (John 15:11 KJV).

No wonder the young in the full tide of life adored Him and left everything to be with Him! And the young today still respond to the lure of adventure and the giving of their all to a cause. That is why the stringency and the sacrifice called for by movements like the Peace Corps have so much appeal.

I can see that Jesus drew men and women into the Kingdom by promising them two things: first, trouble—hardship, danger; and second, joy. But what curious alchemy is this that He can make even danger and hardship seem joyous? He understands things about human nature that we grasp only dimly: few of us are really challenged by the promise of soft living, by an emphasis on me-first, or by a life of easy compromise.

Christ still asks for one's total surrender and then promises His gift of full, overflowing joy. It was that Spirit of joy that I felt in the young people at Estes Park. It was this Spirit that captured my son and turned his life around.

7

Quenching
a Child's Spirit

*A*fter three years of marriage, Len and I are groping for wisdom in relating to each of our children. Gradually we have become aware that family life is God's classroom for shaping us into the kind of people He wants us to be.

God often speaks to me through dreams. Last night, for example, I dreamed I was talking to Jeff, our irrepressible six-year-old. In my right hand was a bottle of what looked like baby aspirin. Jeff and I were having one of our typical confrontations. In the dream, however, I lost my temper and somehow the bottle hit one of his eyes. He cried and to my alarm I saw on my hand fluid from his eye.

The next scene was of Len carrying Jeff into our bedroom, where I was standing by the window. Sitting on his father's knee, Jeff took his forefinger and ran it around his eye socket. I looked and—to my horror—there was no eye there.

"Let's get him to an eye doctor fast!" I urged.

Len's stance was his usual patient tolerance, though now full of sadness. "It's too late. There's no eye there."

I was overcome with grief—then, to my great relief, I woke up.

This morning when I asked the Lord if He was telling me something through this dream, I was led to one of Jesus' teachings in the Sermon on the Mount.

> The eye is the lamp of the body. So, if your eye is sound, your whole body will be full of light.
>
> Matthew 6:22 RSV

Then came His gentle but firm correction to me. I had been putting out, quenching, some of Jeff's light by the way I had been treating him.

Convicted of my sin, I confessed immediately the specific ways I have been quenching the light in Jeff: (1) Through losing my temper (quite inexcusable); (2) dominating him because I'm bigger; (3) not demonstrating enough love for Jeff.

I asked for and received God's forgiveness for these sins. Then I sought out Jeff, hugged him, and asked his forgiveness.

"That's okay, Mom," he said with a grin. Pause. "Can I have Rodney over for lunch today?"

Several weeks later: I dreamed again last night about Jeff. This time he and Chester were tumbling about on the back porch. Suddenly Jeff lost his balance and fell down the steps, his head striking the pavement below.

The next picture was of Jeff being carried off on a stretcher covered with blankets neatly tucked in, with his head heavily bandaged. And in my dream, suddenly I realized how much *I loved this little guy.*

8

Malnutrition of the Spirit

The problems that arise in second marriages are more than I could ever have imagined. Being a new mother to three young children is exhausting, leaving little time for creative writing. There are times when life seems to go gray; I have no zest for anything.

When this happened last week I recognized my problem: *malnutrition of the spirit.*

It was Carol, my friend from California, who had made me aware months ago that spiritual undernourishment can be quite as real as physical starvation. When I first met Carol, it was obvious that she had problems, but not the usual ones. She had a happy marriage; no major troubles with her three children; everything fine economically; no health difficulties.

But she felt tired all the time from the daily routine. "Nothing is much fun anymore," she had said. "I have so little energy that no undertaking seems worth attempting. What's wrong with me?"

An hour and much talk later, I had a sudden inspiration: could it be that Carol's inner spirit was starving to death?

Taking up my Bible, I turned to the Old Testament story of Daniel. I read to her about how Daniel was in exile in the king's palace. "His windows being open in his chamber toward Jerusalem, he kneeled upon his knees three times a day, and prayed, and gave thanks before his God, as he did aforetime" (Daniel 6:10 KJV).

"We have three meals a day," I suggested. "Perhaps we need spiritual food three times a day too."

"But what *is* spiritual food? And how do you take it?" Carol asked.

"Jesus said that His words are spirit and life indeed. He used metaphor upon metaphor to tell us that His Spirit is our life substance. He described himself as 'living water' and 'the bread of life.' Meeting Him in Scripture is like an intravenous feeding from His Spirit to our spirit," I replied.

"So," I challenged Carol, "would you be willing to try spiritual food in the form of life-giving Bible verses three times a day for one month?"

At a Christian bookstore Carol found an "Inspiration Box" of paper capsules, each containing a verse of Scripture. They were to be taken daily as spiritual vitamins. (This word "vitamin" means "life substance.")

Later, with another spiritually undernourished friend, we decided that an additional blessing came when we took the time ourselves to dig through Scripture and put together a homemade card file of spiritual vitamins.

So last week I produced a "Vitamin Box" of dozens of favorite passages for my new family. I used a concordance and looked up words such as *strength, food, bread, water, hunger,* and *thirst.* Other cards were culled from Christ's own words. Now before blessing the food at each meal, we pass the box, and one of the children chooses a card to read aloud. The nourishment is most effective when the life-giving words of Scripture are memorized and so become the permanent possessions of mind and heart.

> But they that wait upon the Lord shall renew their strength; they shall mount up with wings as eagles; they shall run, and not be weary; and they shall walk, and not faint.
>
> Isaiah 40:31 KJV

> For the Lord disciplines the man he loves. . . . So up with your listless hands! Strengthen your weak knees! And make straight paths for your feet.
>
> Hebrews 12:6, 12–13, MOFFATT

> Oh that men would praise the Lord for his goodness, and for his wonderful works to the children of men! For he satisfieth the long-ing soul, and filleth the hungry soul with goodness.
>
> Psalm 107:8–9 KJV

> . . . My grace is sufficient for thee: for my strength is made perfect in weakness.
>
> 2 Corinthians 12:9 KJV

By saturating my mind with these and other verses, I find that the grayness lifts, the spirit is infused with spiritual food, and I am ready to meet any difficulty that comes along.

9
Early Morning Time

> Awake my soul, and with the sun
> Thy daily stage of duty run;
> Shake off dull sloth, and joyful rise
> To pay the morning sacrifice!
>
> Shine on me, Lord, new life impart,
> Fresh ardors kindle in my heart;
> One ray of Thine all-quickening light
> Dispels the clouds and dark of night.
>
> Thomas Ken (1637–1711)

As Len and I arise at 6:00 A.M. this morning, I find the above verses help move me from "dull sloth" to "fresh ardors." Then in Psalm 5, I read:

Give ear to my words, O Lord, consider my meditation. Hearken unto the voice of my cry. . . . My voice shalt thou hear in the morning, O Lord; in the morning will I direct my prayer unto thee, and will look up.

Psalm 5:1–3 KJV

God, who created heaven and earth, will hear *my* voice? The King of the universe will consider *my* meditation? Oh, thank You, Lord, for the undreamed-of opportunity of this audience with the King! Anyone who has a favor to ask of an earthly monarch has no chance of having his request granted until he makes his wish known to the king. That *could* be second-hand—generally is, in protocol-bound human societies. What a privilege to have an audience in person! Yet this is the status and the honor You allow each of us, Lord.

Even more privileged is he so in favor with the King that he is allowed as long as he wishes to be with the One he loves, listen to Him, watch Him, bask in His presence. In earthly courts, such a one would be considered favored indeed, and the courts we're invited to enter are of an "infinite majesty." Just to say "Thank You" seems inadequate. This morning I make it a welling, swelling gratitude!

10

Subject One
to Another

*T*his week I've been focusing my thoughts and prayers on the fifth chapter of Ephesians.

> Wives be subject—be submissive and adapt yourselves—to your own husbands as [a service] to the Lord. For the husband is head of the wife as Christ is the Head of the church. . . . As the church is subject to Christ, so let wives also be subject in everything to their husbands.
>
> Ephesians 5:22–24 AMPLIFIED

Like many women, I've struggled with conflicting emotions over the current emphasis on "submission." Especially when I hear of a case, as I did last week, of a husband who used this passage in Ephesians to intimidate his wife and force her to accept and condone his own adultery with another woman. An extreme situation, of course, but one of many instances where the basic truth of Scripture is violated or distorted when taken out of context.

For example, the admonition "Wives, submit to your husbands" is coupled in Ephesians with, "Husbands, love your wives, as Christ loved the church and gave Himself up for her" (v. 25). Yet this complementary verse is frequently overlooked.

This week's Bible focus was promoted by a letter:

"I am having a mighty struggle with my role as a Christian wife," the woman wrote. "Something inside of me literally rebels at the words—obey, submit, subject! At times I have considered the apostle Paul to be a male chauvinist. Also, I can't believe that my loving heavenly Father, as I personally know Him, would want me to be as completely and blindly submissive as these Scriptures seem to indicate.

"I realize my resentment and selfishness is sin, yet when I try to submit to my husband, I end up feeling angry and hypocritical. Or like a spiritless dumb animal. How do I understand and accept this teaching?"

To answer this question, I've taken time to review my own relationship as a wife to Len, study the Ephesians chapter, then talk and pray some more with my husband.

When we were first married, Len suggested that I assume spiritual responsibility for our home. This seemed wrong to me. It went against a number of scriptural teachings. Also I doubted that Len's two sons would respond to this; they would perhaps see religion as "a woman's thing." In fact, Chester, the elder son, who is gifted in all sports, sees God the Father primarily through his own athletic father. Once Len and I began to search the Bible together in the early mornings, he saw for himself that he should take spiritual leadership of our home and did so.

But there's more. As we study Ephesians 5, we're beginning to believe that this may be one of the most misinterpreted chapters in the New Testament. Nor do we believe that St. Paul was any kind of male chauvinist.

Much light is shed when we investigate the background against which Paul was teaching. He had come out of Judaism, a patriarchal system where women were considered their husbands' property. Still, Jewish women were better off than most. In the other countries around the Mediterranean basin of Paul's day, wives had no political or social status whatever, were allowed no education, no activity beyond the home. In the Greek world, for instance, groups of single young women were trained to provide the social and sex life of Greek husbands whose wives stayed at home, did the menial tasks, and cared for the children.

In Ephesians, chapters four through six, Paul is speaking out against this immoral system and is trying to teach new Ephesian Christians how they should relate to one another. It is only against this pagan backdrop that we can see how revolutionary Paul's "Husbands, love your wives" was! Not only was Paul not against women, he, like his Master before him, was teaching that women are equally children of the Father and as such are to be respected and beloved. At that time this was a radically new approach to women.

In the end we're discovering that the hub upon which the Ephesian "submission" passages turn is the statement that introduces them: "Be subject to one another out of reverence for Christ" (Ephesians 5:21 AMPLIFIED). This is the irreducible minimum of Paul's instructions to all Christians—male or female.

What is coming out of Len's and my seeking prayers on this subject can be described as a triangle of authority more than a pecking order. God is at the apex of the triangle; the husband and wife are equally positioned at the lower corners. Thus both mates are equal in His sight, equally beloved by Him, equally committed to each other and to Him.

We're finding "Be subject to one another out of reverence for Christ" to be intensely practical. It means a spirit of mutual respect, a willingness to listen. It means giving—and sometimes giving in—on the part of both of us, since sometimes God gives His direction through Len, at other times through me. Most importantly, at the peak of the triangle God Himself has to be acknowledged as the final Authority in the home.

In thinking further about the subject this morning, I realize that I want for our home everything in that Ephesians chapter. I want Len to be its spiritual head. I want him to be a husband whom I can love and trust and submit to in the biblical sense. I want him to love me as Jesus loves the Church, to love me as he would love his own body. I also want to "respect, reverence, honor, love, and esteem him exceedingly."

Section Two
Adventuresome
Living

*T*ravel is often called "the door to adventure." Catherine and I had our share of this kind of excitement. During the early years of our marriage we visited Uganda, Kenya, the Holy Land, drove through central Europe, painted with oils on the beaches of Bora Bora and Moorea in the South Pacific, shared stories with missionaries in such remote places as Tonga, Fiji, and Tahiti, ministered to groups in Samoa and Australia.

Yet the real adventure for us was always spiritual: testing scriptural truths, exploring different kinds of prayer, sharing in fellowship groups, teaching together from the Bible. The base for the first five years of our marriage was Chappaqua, New York. When Northern winters caused increasing congestion of Catherine's lungs, we moved to Boynton Beach, Florida, in November 1964.

The first of our children to marry was Peter who met Edith Wallis at Princeton Theological Seminary. They were married on May 29, 1966, and their daughter, Mary Elizabeth Marshall, was born on March 1, 1969.

During these years life was tumultuous, demanding, often exhausting. With God in charge of our lives, there was the never-ending suspense of wondering what He had in store for us next.

LL

I

The Prayer of Agreement

I am impressed this morning with the power in a Scripture verse about prayer.

When my son Peter accepted an invitation to give a speech in Kansas City, I had a telephone call from a dentist in that city who was on the sponsoring committee. This man asked me to pray for the meeting and that Peter's message would be God's topic for this particular audience at this particular time.

The dentist and I decided to claim the promise of Jesus in Matthew 18:19–20 RSV:

"If two of you agree on earth about anything they ask, it will be done for them by my Father in heaven. For where two or three are gathered in my name, there am I in the midst of them."

In heartfelt accord, my caller and I asked God that His word only be spoken at the upcoming gathering.

Peter's talk was in the newly decorated ballroom of the largest hotel in Kansas City, with six hundred people in attendance. The audience were both Christians and non-Christians, a cross section of civic Kansas City.

Len and I learned later that just before Peter was to speak a black man with a powerful voice sang "There Is a Balm in Gilead." This got to everyone, especially Peter.

On the table beside him were the notes of the prepared speech, which he had in fact planned to use. After hearing the song, he shoved aside his papers, rose, and picked up the theme of the song for his talk. For one hour and fifteen minutes he laid out before that Kansas City audience Jesus Christ as *the* "balm in Gilead."

The room was so quiet (according to the dentist) that not even the usual coughing and respiratory upheavals were in evidence. A doctor friend, not particularly religious, who was there as the guest of the dentist, told him afterwards, "I've never witnessed or heard anything like it. It was so quiet that I was almost afraid to breathe."

I asked the dentist, "But, speaking that long extemporaneously, didn't Peter ramble or repeat himself?"

"Not once," he answered. "However you tie it, Catherine, when anyone can hold six hundred people *that* attentive for an hour and a quarter—that had to be God."

What neither Peter nor the dentist knows is that "There Is a Balm in Gilead" was one of the favorite songs of Peter's father. He had sung it in a quartet during his seminary days. He sometimes sang it as a duet in Westminster Church in Atlanta. When he was pastor of the

New York Avenue Church in Washington, it was one of the favorite numbers of Charlie Beaschler's great massed choirs. Now, through that singer in Kansas City, God has used it again to bring His message to a hurting world.

2

Happiness Is . . .

As I've been pondering the subject of happiness this morning—an elusive and seemingly unattainable state for so many—I am led to these words of Jesus:

> If any man would come after me, let him deny himself and take up
> his cross and follow me. For whoever would save his life will lose it,
> and whoever loses his life for my sake will find it.
>
> Matthew 16:24–25 RSV

I believe the secret of happiness lies imbedded in those words, painful though they appear to be. How else explain radiant people like the young man who sat in our living room and described how his six-year-old boy had died in his arms from leukemia. Today this man finds fulfillment in giving himself totally to helping college students. Or the woman I visited recently whose husband had turned out to be a homosexual and demanded a divorce. Some years later, this woman also lost her eyesight. Yet she is a cheerful, loving person, fully self-supporting.

You might say that such people almost have a right to be unhappy. That they are not, lies in the way they spend themselves for others.

I have observed that when any of us embarks on the pursuit of happiness for ourselves, it eludes us. Often I've asked myself why. It must be because happiness comes to us only as a dividend. When we become absorbed in something demanding and worthwhile above and beyond ourselves, happiness seems to be there as a by-product of the self-giving.

That should not be a startling truth, yet I'm surprised at how few people understand and accept it. Have we made a god of happiness? Have we been brainwashed by ads assuring us "Happiness is . . ."— usually a big, shiny, new gadget?

Perhaps our national preoccupation with happiness dates from these words in the Declaration of Independence:

> . . . All men are . . . endowed by their Creator with certain unalienable rights, [and] among these are life, liberty and *the pursuit of happiness* [italics added].

Now, I have always had immense admiration for Thomas Jefferson, author of these words. And until recently I never questioned them. But (and my apologies to you, Mr. Jefferson) I do question them as I see more and more people interpret "the pursuit of happiness" as a license to grab for power or money or physical pleasure.

The truth, as I see it, is that not one of us has "an unalienable right" to anything, not even to life itself. We did nothing to bring about our birth, and we are dependent for the next breath we draw on the grace of God. How arrogant and ungrateful we must seem to our Creator when we demand our "rights."

I think of Mary and Harold Brinig—a remarkable couple who found the true basis of happiness some years ago. Having moved to Chicago where they had no friends, they became irritable with each other and unhappy. While seeking help from the Bible one day, they were struck by these words of Jesus:

> You did not choose me, but I chose you and appointed you that you should go and bear fruit and that your fruit should abide. . . .
>
> John 15:16 RSV

Somehow that passage was like light penetrating their darkness: much of their unhappiness, they realized, was caused by self-centeredness. Could Jesus be choosing them for service? But practically speaking, how could this happen in a big city like Chicago?

The first person they encountered after this revelation was the waitress who served them in a nearby restaurant. She apologized for giving slow service, admitted she was new in the city and miserable. They invited her to visit them in their apartment after work.

"You did not choose me, but I chose you. . . ." A widower in the next apartment was the second person they befriended. Soon a dozen people were meeting together once a week for conversation and prayer.

Out of these meetings grew a project called Adventures in Friendship. Before long, scores of people were involved in seeking the lonely and the shut-ins throughout the whole area. Needless to say, Mary and Harold Brinig had become so absorbed in the needs of others that their own life was enriched beyond anything I can describe. Happiness found them.

This Chicago experience prepared the Brinigs for a thirty-five-year team ministry at the Marble Collegiate Church in New York City that resulted in spiritually rejuvenated lives for thousands of people, including my husband, Len.

3

The Power of Let

While reading a manuscript by Mrs. John Peters (wife of the founder of World Neighbors), I was intrigued by one episode in particular. Losing his footing in the bathroom, her husband struck his head on the ceramic soap dish. One ear was almost severed and he was bleeding profusely when Mrs. Peters heard his cries and came to his aid.

Despite her shock at the sight of so much blood, the Spirit took over and enabled her to speak with authority. She heard herself saying, "Let the bleeding stop immediately. Let there be no infection. Let there be no pain. Let there be no scarring."

Mrs. Peters made no comment on the experience other than to report that, gloriously, the bleeding stopped. There was no infection.

Almost no pain. No scars. But something about these "Lets" stuck like glue to my mind.

I realized that it was the same word God had used in creating our world. *"Let* there be light,". . . and so on.

Jesus to His disciples:

> *Let* your light so shine before men, that they may see your good works, and glorify your Father which is in heaven.
>
> Matthew 5:16 KJV
>
> And if the house is worthy, *let* your peace come upon it; but if it is not worthy, *let* your peace return to you.
>
> Matthew 10:13 RSV

Paul used it too:

> *Let* this mind be in you, which was also in Christ Jesus.
>
> Philippians 2:5 KJV

What, I wondered, is the significance of this word for us?

Author Harold Hill gave me the missing insight. "'Let' is a word of tremendous faith with volumes of meaning poured into it," he told me. "It *assumes* the total love and good will of the Father. It *assumes* that heaven is crammed with good gifts that the Father desires to give His children. The 'let' is saying, 'Father, I give to You permission to do so-and-so for us down here on earth. I allow it.'"

It also assumes an almost preposterous humility on God's part— that He should wait for our permission to bestow wonderful gifts on us! How amazing!

Worlds of meaning behind this three-letter word . . . *let.*

4

The Poverty Complex

I'm going through one of those "money anxiety" periods this morning, Lord, so I know I've taken my eyes off You and placed them squarely on worldly matters.

The sad thing is that I know better. Only the other day I was expressing my incredulity over a famous financier who committed suicide when his wealth diminished from fifty million to ten million. It seemed inconceivable that a man could feel desperate about money when he still possessed ten million dollars. Wealth, clearly, is a matter of attitude.

So once again I go through the process of replacing fear with faith in connection with Your provision.

First, I need to remind myself that You control all of earth's ma-

terial resources. Most of us do not really believe this. Yet from cover
to cover the Bible declares it:

The earth is the Lord's and the fulness thereof. . . .
Psalm 24:1 KJV
But my God shall supply all your need according to his riches. . . .
Philippians 4:19 KJV

If I truly believe that I am a child of a King, then my fear will
disappear. Worrying would be the sure sign that I did not believe
God's ownership of earth's resources. To think myself a pauper is to
deny either the King's riches or my being His beloved child.

Second, I can think about Mary Welch. Born in a log cabin on a
run-down farm in west Texas, even after she became a Christian she
found it difficult to shed her poverty complex. A turning point for her
came when she was in St. Paul, Minnesota, on a speaking trip as the
guest of a wealthy woman. As she was preparing to take a bath before
dinner, she drew her customary three inches of water in the tub.

Her hostess happened to look into the tub. "You're not intending
to take a bath in that tiny amount of water?"

"Why not? That's all I ever use."

"This isn't Texas, Mary," her hostess chided her. "There's no shortage of water here. Minnesota has ten *thousand* lakes."

Mary realized that she had just gotten a sharp insight about herself.
She watched the water nearly fill the tub. Then she lathered herself
with soap—marveling at all she was wasting. That night before she
went to sleep she asked God to register His Perfect Adequacy on her
subconscious and clear out all her deep-rooted beliefs in shortages.

Soon after, Mary realized that even her skinny, ninety-pound body
looked like a shortage of woman. She took a piece of soft soap and, in
a full-length mirror, drew an outline of her ideal measurements. Then
she packed most of her size-three dresses to send to an orphanage.

Her mother caught her at the packing and didn't approve at all.
"You've never had much. You worked too hard to get those clothes to
give them away. Besides, suppose you *don't* gain weight?"

But Mary realized that she could not pray for one thing and make provisions for another. Furthermore, she had discovered what she calls the "law of the Golden Initiative": the secret of receiving is to give— even out of poverty. In fact, the more sunk we are in visions of lack, the greater need we have to start giving.

So the dresses went off to the orphanage. "And within that year," Mary reports, "I measured exactly what I had pictured and prepared for—size nine."

The third thing I'm to do is to remind myself of that moment of decision I faced some weeks after Peter Marshall's death in 1949. The trustees of his church gave me a bleak financial report of how little insurance money there was. They advised me to take a full-time job to support Peter John and myself.

You, Lord, encouraged me to write, with the promise that if I trusted You, all my needs would be met. I took Your challenge and how greatly have You blessed me! Thank you, Lord. Praise You! Forgive me for my lack of faith.

5

Forward,
Like Gideon!

*T*his morning, Len and I dragged ourselves out of bed at 6:00 A.M. for our morning prayer time. After the long drive from Evergreen Farm in Virginia to southern Florida, I'm exhausted. Our suitcases are still packed. But there's a meeting of our church committee on Christian education this afternoon that Len insists we attend.

I'm fighting off resentment as well as fatigue. I want to get back to my writing. Meetings drain me. Bore me. Len wants us to teach a class on the Holy Spirit this winter to a group that is resistant to what is happening across the country today, frightened by the excesses of some of the "Jesus people," by speaking in tongues and so on. Len looks at this class as an adventure. I'm full of doubts as to whether we can handle it.

Is it coincidence that I have been reading the Book of Judges? Today it was the story of Gideon. Such fascinating reading! So jam-packed full of truths and insights!

For instance, Gideon certainly had no idea that he was anyone special in God's sight or in man's. He lived at a low point in Israel's history when the people had forsaken Jehovah and were worshiping idols.

Yet God sent an angel to Gideon with the message, "The Lord is with you, you mighty man of [fearless] courage" (Judges 6:12 AMPLIFIED).

There's immense humor in this greeting. For the "mighty man of courage" was at that moment hiding out in a winepress for fear of the Midianites.

And his reaction to the angel's appearance was doubt and confusion. "If the Lord is with us, why is all this befallen us?" (v. 13).

The answer was a strange one. The angel did not rebuke Gideon for answering back with unbelief. Instead, he repeated, "Go in this your might, and you shall save Israel from the hand of Midian. Have I not sent you?" (v. 14).

Again Gideon sounds like anything but a hero. He replies, in effect, "Who, me? Save Israel? Surely you must be kidding. My clan is the poorest in Israel and I'm the least in my father's house, the youngest son, the one everyone picks on."

The Lord's answer is, "Surely, I will be with you, and you shall smite the Midianites as one man" (v. 16).

Only after the angel disappears does Gideon seem to realize that he has actually been in the presence of an angel. His reaction to this, characteristically, is downbeat all the way. He might have been thrilled and begun praising God. Instead, he says, "Alas, O Lord God! For now I have seen the Angel of the Lord face to face!" (v. 22).

Never on God's side, however, is there anything but patient understanding of Gideon's doubt and unbelief. "Peace be to you; do not fear, you shall not die" (v. 23).

Then begins a series of clear-cut instructions from the Lord. First, Gideon is to tear down two idols.

The "mighty man of courage" obeys, but does it at night because he's so scared of his own clan, even of his father and brothers.

In fact, his father sticks up for him before the townspeople.

But Gideon is full of doubt still. Only after elaborate further signs and reassurances from Jehovah will he consent to take command of the Israelite forces. And then the point of the story becomes clear: it is God's strength and His alone that delivers us. For God persuades Gideon to reduce his warriors from 22,000 to 300. And it is this small army that routs the Midianites.

The clear message for today that I receive from this reading is that God is going to show me that I can rely on Him alone—for physical strength as for every other need. So thank You, Lord, for the meeting I will go to this afternoon, hence no nap today. Thank You for the challenge of teaching a class on the Holy Spirit. Full speed ahead, O Gideon!

6

Small Needs

After the Bible study I gave last week on praying for all our needs, no matter how small, one woman took sharp issue with me.

"Asking for small things is being selfish," she remonstrated, "and self-centered prayers just aren't answered. I think we should pray only about *spiritual* needs. Besides, the God who runs the universe can't be bothered with individual wishes."

I could only reply that this was not Jesus' viewpoint as presented in the Gospels: both by teaching and by action He impressed upon us that no need is too trivial for His attention.

I've combed Scripture for examples and there are many, such as: The wine needed at a wedding feast (John 2:1–11); a dying sparrow (Matthew 10:29); a lost lamb (Luke 15:3–7).

These vignettes, scattered through the Gospels like little patches of gold dust, say to us, "No creaturely need is outside the scope of prayer."

As if to emphasize the same thought, the apostle Paul adds:

> Do not fret or have any anxiety about anything, but in every circumstance and in everything by prayer and petition [definite requests] with thanksgiving continue to make your wants known to God.
>
> Philippians 4:6 AMPLIFIED

Now obviously not all our human wants are genuine needs. Moreover, we are often so selfish and shortsighted that the granting of some wants would not be good for us. But I believe that Scripture invites us to talk over all our concerns and dreams with our Father, then leave the outcome to His wisdom.

Just before Christmas we had a wonderful example of His loving involvement in the everyday-ness of life. My son Peter was laboring to build an elaborate miniature horse stable for his daughter, Mary Elizabeth. Hour after hour, he closeted himself in the basement putting it together. Especially time-consuming was the process of covering the roof with tiny shingles of almost paper-thin plywood. As the laborious work of positioning and gluing proceeded, it became apparent that he was going to run out of shingles.

Peter called all manner of hobby stores in the area. Nobody had any.

He even called the company in Texas that made the shingles. Yes, they could get them to him in time by special plane service for about $100. Too costly.

Finally, Peter found a hobby store up the road that had half of one package. The owner's wife had been using them for some project and had that many left. This was still not enough to complete the roof, but Peter decided to pick up those that were available.

As he drove off I breathed up a quiet little prayer about this. Immediately I had a mental picture—a little drama really—of Peter walking into the hobby store and the owner saying, "I have a surprise for you. I found another package of those shingles."

Peter came back home beaming. What I had "seen" as I prayed was exactly what had happened. He had more than enough to finish the roof.

A very small prayer request for what many would consider a superficial need. Yet this little episode gave all of us a heartwarming glimpse of the Father's careful provision for the small details of our lives—and of the adventure He means each moment in His world to be!

7

Homemade Bread

I am troubled about a quality of blandness in our nation today, a lack of creativity. It's apparent in our leaders. Most gear their lives to television ratings, are afraid to take stands on issues. Movies and stage plays focus on sex and violence, with little originality. Sex so dominates advertising and the arts that it has become commonplace, almost boring.

Jesus lashed out at the spiritless quality in the people of His time:

> I know thy works, that thou art neither cold nor hot: I would thou
> wert cold or hot. So, then, because thou art lukewarm, and neither
> cold nor hot, I will spew thee out of my mouth.
>
> Revelation 3:15–16 KJV

One of our new neighbors is no longer trapped in a bland way of life. Yet for the first twelve years of her marriage, Cynthia felt she was losing her identity in an endless procession of social events and chauffeuring of children.

During one cocktail party, Cynthia decided to limit herself to ginger ale and made some discoveries—not especially pleasant: "I saw our crowd through new eyes," she told me. "No one was really saying anything. Most sentences were never even finished. There was a lot of laughter over—well, nothing at all. All at once I began to ask questions about what we call 'the good life.'

"What was so good about it?"

"But," she continued, "what was I to do? If my husband and I ducked those invitations, we'd be thought snobbish and eventually dropped. But if we went, we would have to drink, otherwise how could we stand the emptiness?"

In a search for answers, Cynthia set aside an hour each day for meditation. As she did this over a period of weeks there came to her the realization that she was being met in this quiet hour, at her point of need, by something more than her own thoughts and her own psyche, by Someone who loved her and who insisted that His love must be passed on to her family and her friends.

Cynthia began to bake bread regularly, finding this ancient female ritual deeply satisfying. "You can't imagine how many enemies I slay and repressions I get rid of as I knead that bread," she says.

Instead of letting the children dash away from the dinner table for television, the evening meal has become a time for family sharing. Family Game Night once a week has become a creative substitute for television.

A new strength developed in Cynthia in regard to her children. I have heard her tell her astonished eleven-year-old that he is going to walk to Little League one way each practice day, and calmly state to her nine-year-old daughter that she certainly is not going to buy her any "training" bras.

"I've discovered that real love for our children has to go beyond catering to their every whim—or we turn them into tyrannical little princes and princesses," Cynthia said. "They, too, have to find their own inner resources. And how can they, if I do for them the things that they could do for themselves?"

Recognizing that some of her friends were as bored as she with the typical cocktail party, she began experimenting with some new types of entertaining. One evening after a buffet supper, a hand-picked group listened spellbound to a play on the radio, "The Murder Trial of William Palmer, Surgeon." Cynthia had supplied each guest with a paperback copy of the play to follow as they listened. The evening was a big hit, especially with the men.

"I realized one day that my church had little more meaning for me than did our country club," Cynthia said. "I called our pastor and asked if there was a Bible study."

That's what brought Cynthia and her husband to our house, where eight couples were already meeting twice a month to find ways to relate the Bible to some everyday problems we were all facing. Out of this experience has come a new level of shared concerns for us all and the exciting discovery of answers sought out together.

As I ponder Cynthia's story, I've concluded that we don't have to settle for blandness in life; God, who is the Author of creativity, is ready to make a dull life adventuresome the moment we allow His Holy Spirit to go to work inside us.

Section Three _____
Christian
Growth _____

*T*here is a misconception in the minds of many believers that successful communicators of the faith speak from some Mt. Olympus of perfection—that it is only because these Christian superstars have overcome their faults and weaknesses that they are able to minister to others in a mighty way.

Not true. Those most used of God often have struggled or are struggling with one or more major weaknesses. It is often just because of a weakness that these people have much to share.

Dr. Norman Vincent Peale frankly admits that only due to his own fears and doubts and tensions was he able to minister so effectively to others with similar problems. A study of Christian leaders down through the ages reveals that most of them battled major weaknesses.

So it was with Catherine. The Lord gave her major gifts in the area of communication that catapulted her into the public eye. But when people tried to place her on a pedestal, she refused, knowing that God alone deserves to be exalted. Instead, she wrote openly about her struggles, her mistakes, her flaws.

In her journals she was ruthless with herself. The following excerpts indicate how hard she struggled to overcome certain weaknesses, how seriously she took the matter of our need to grow spiritually.

A lesson learned was an inadequately thought-through novel she began in 1969 and abandoned two-and-a-half years later. It was titled Gloria. The loss of time and energy on this manuscript weighed on Catherine for years.

LL

I

Dealing with a Major Mistake

*L*ast week I needed to be alone for a few days to think and pray. The mistake I made in deciding to write the novel *Gloria* has shaken my confidence. The shelved manuscript is like a death in the family.

What went wrong?

I needed to find some answers about this—and about other troubling areas in my life. So I made arrangements to spend two days at the Cenacle, a Roman Catholic Retreat House several miles away in Lantana, Florida. Len dropped me off Sunday at 8:00 P.M.

The next morning after breakfast I sat for a while in a lawn chair out under an ancient mango tree. Through the curving trunks of the coconut palms I had a glimpse of the Intracoastal Waterway. The grounds were alive with bird calls.

A sound new to me was the creaking of the tall, tall bamboo that borders part of the property. The bamboo, too, was ancient. The slender branches writhed and creaked as they rubbed against one another in the barely perceptible breeze. The creaking reminded me of the grating of a long-unused hinge, as of a door being opened after many years. The foliage was still delicate and lacy as it was when the bamboo was young.

Leaf patterns were all across the grass. Squirrels raced up and down trees. A cardinal kept whistling, "Cheer! Cheer!"

I had thought that I wanted guidance on certain family matters and whether there was some way to resurrect *Gloria.* But when I talked briefly with Sister Forman at breakfast, her advice was to seek Christ and Him alone and let Him decide what He wanted to talk to me about.

That morning the first thought dropped into my mind was the single word *edification.* "Think on edification," He seemed to be saying, "what builds the members of the family up in love, perfecting them into the body of Christ."

The focus throughout the morning was largely on my home situation. (Perhaps the conclusion to be drawn is that it's essential that I get this right with Christ before I can write *anything* worthwhile.)

Soon I found myself turning to the book of John. As I read, the Holy Spirit showed me that I had fallen hook, line, and sinker for one of Satan's oldest and most-used tricks: looking steadily at the difficulty instead of at Jesus. I had listened, really paid attention to Old Scratch's suggestions—every one of them, I fear—as to the size and intractability of my problems. The Comforter told me that all of this had been Satan's technique for discouraging me unduly and that I must *never* fall for this temptation again.

Next I was shown that my husband, my children, and my grandchildren are not mine, but God's. He's not only as concerned as I am for them, but loves them far more than I ever could. Therefore, I was to take my possessive, self-centered hands off—strictly off. So, in an act of relinquishment, I did this.

Then came a beautiful touch. I was reading in the Psalms when suddenly these words leapt from the page:

> The Lord will perfect that which concerns me . . . forsake not the works of Your own hands.
>
> Psalm 138:8 AMPLIFIED

I could—and did—claim this promise promptly for my family. Years ago the Lord began a work in these lives. It's His business to perfect what He started. He has promised that He will. I've claimed and accepted that promise. It's as good as done. My heart is steadily rejoicing. Weights and weights have been lifted from me.

The focus that afternoon turned from my home situation to my failure with *Gloria.* What do You have to tell me about this, Lord?

I was led to this passages in Numbers:

> . . . the people . . . spoke against God and against Moses, and said, "Why have you brought us up out of Egypt to die in the desert? There is no bread! There is no water! And we detest this miserable food!"
>
> Then the Lord sent venomous snakes among them; they bit the people and many Israelites died. The people came to Moses and said, "We sinned when we spoke against the Lord and against you. Pray that the Lord will take the snakes away from us." So Moses prayed for the people.
>
> The Lord said to Moses, "Make a snake and put it up on a pole; anyone who is bitten can look at it and live." So Moses made a bronze snake and put it up on a pole. Then when anyone was bitten by a snake and looked at the bronze snake, he lived.
>
> Numbers 21:4–9 NIV

It didn't take long for me to get the point: God told Moses that the people were to take that which had hurt them and lift it up to Him.

He would then turn even a snake into blessing and victory. Thus the "snake" in our life can be redeemed and turned to power.

In this way does God deal with our mistakes and sins. I had made a mistake in undertaking the novel *Gloria.* I had not heeded the advice of experts like Elizabeth Sherrill and Len; even my mother had expressed strong reservations. But God would find a way to turn a bad experience into good.

Even more to the point: when any one of us has made a wrong (or even doubtful) turning in our lives through arrogance or lack of trust or impatience or fear—or what not—God will show us a way out. Therefore, I am to turn off all negative thoughts about this wrong decision and accept fully my situation as it is now, as God's will for me now. I am to place the present situation in His hands for Him to use fully for my spiritual growth and for the "edification" of all concerned. Further, I am to do this joyfully.

2

The Servant Role

The message I am getting today from Jesus is the servant role that He wants to play in the lives of every one of us. The following passages reveal to me the extent of His passion to *serve* us because He loves us so much:

> . . . the Son of man came not to be waited on but to serve, and to give His life as a ransom for many. . . .
>
> Matthew 20:28 AMPLIFIED
>
> . . . I am in your midst as one who serves.
>
> Luke 22:27 AMPLIFIED

In the early days of my walk with Him, when I was experimenting day by day with hearing the Inner Voice, I had a hard time believing that His guidance was for *my* benefit, never His own. I still can hardly grasp this.

When He wrapped a towel around his waist, poured water into a basin, and began to wash his disciples' feet (see John 13:4–5), Simon Peter objected that this was beneath the dignity of the Master. *We* the disciples are to be the servants, I want to insist along with Peter. But Jesus answered him, "If I do not wash you, you have no part in me."

This is a stunning and stupendous thought. Unless I can believe in *this much* love for me, unless I can and will accept Him with faith as my servant as well as my God, unless I truly know that it's *my* good He seeks, not His glory (He already has all of that He can use for all eternity), *then I cannot have his companionship.*

What an amazing revelation!

3

Why Do We Judge Others?

I am determined to dig in on the matter of my critical nature. I do not like it. It's negative; yes, often destructive. Jesus warned us not to be judgmental. So did Paul:

> Then let us no more pass judgment on one another, but rather decide never to put a stumbling block or hindrance in the way.
>
> Romans 14:13 RSV

I have tried to excuse myself by saying that one must evaluate situations and people. It won't wash. It still comes out judging, a haughty superiority, which is the opposite of love.

With Jesus' help I want to go back to my childhood to see if I can find the root cause for this fault of mine:

He is showing me a little girl who was supersensitive in the sense that she would rather die than be laughed at or found unacceptable by her peers, and most of all, by the adults around her. When she didn't make friends as quickly as other children, she tried to persuade herself that she was superior to others her age.

She got by with this superiority syndrome in school because she received top grades, especially in writing and speech courses. She yearned to be like classmates who were outgoing, witty, and popular, but since she had none of these personality traits, she convinced herself that these were lesser qualities while those of the mind and spirit were somehow on a higher plane.

When she left her small hometown for college, nothing changed in her approach to other people. Because she felt inferior socially, she looked with secret disapproval at those who danced, played cards, and went to drinking parties, all denied to her as a preacher's child.

Superiority breeds contempt. And contempt breeds criticalness. And my criticalness cut me off from other people. Even when I said nothing, made no comment at all, people would tell me they could feel my unkind judgment of them. I was miserable about this quality in me, yet trapped by it.

Along with all this, ironically enough, went an acute sensitivity to any criticalness of me. The Holy Spirit pointed out to me how *deeply* the least tiny bit of unacceptance rankles, causing a wound that festers on, year after year. Incidents, so small that a healthy reaction on my part should have been amusement and then prompt dismissal of the incident from mind, are remembered—still with an emotional sting attached—years later.

For instance . . . soon after I was married to Peter Marshall, I remember a woman friend commenting about my hands, "Well, they aren't beautiful, but at least they're capable-looking."

The pronouncement that my hands weren't pretty has stuck; ever since it made me reluctant to have a manicurist do my nails.

This is, of course, acute oversensitivity, which, in turn, is the sure sign of acute self-centeredness . . . the same hypersensitivity and self-protectiveness that had led me to take refuge in an assumed superiority to others—with the accompanying right to stand in judgment on them.

Being oversensitive, I am quick to pick it up in others and relate to it. Once when a judge at the Junior Miss Pageant in Mobile, Alabama, I found myself intrigued by the contestant with the highest academic average of all fifty girls. When she came to the five judges for her ten-minute interview, I watched her with deep interest.

One question asked her was: "If you could pick out one person in any field of endeavor in our world today whom you admire most, whom would you pick?"

She hesitated a moment and then said loud and clear, "Jesus Christ."

Two of the judges responded almost simultaneously, "Oh, we mean a living person."

The girl felt rebuked. Her eyes filled with tears; she choked up and never could get herself under control during the rest of the interview. I ached for her. I wanted to hug her and tell her I loved her reply, that to me, as to her, Jesus *was* a living person.

Later, though, I wondered if her extreme sensitivity had caused her to put all her efforts into getting top grades—thereby avoiding, as I had, the far riskier confrontation of equal-to-equal.

How do we sensitive, critical people deal with our condition? I had one very direct answer from the Lord recently after I had loosed a blast of angry criticism at one of our national leaders at the luncheon table. God said to me, "Do not criticize at all" (1 Corinthians 4:5 MOFFATT). You spread negativism around you and pollute your own atmosphere when you do so. Turn your criticism and your indignation to good use by praying for that leader right now."

A good handle for me to grasp!

4

A Fast
on Criticalness

The Lord continues to deal with me about my critical spirit, convicting me that I have been wrong to judge any person or situation:

> Do not judge, or you too will be judged. For in the same way you judge others, you will be judged, and with the measure you use, it will be measured to you.
>
> Matthew 7:1–2 NIV

One morning last week He gave me an assignment: *for one day I was to go on a "fast" from criticism. I was not to criticize anybody about anything.*

Into my mind crowded all the usual objections. "But then what happens to value judgments? You Yourself, Lord, spoke of 'righteous judgment.' How could society operate without standards and limits?"

All such resistance was brushed aside. "Just obey Me without questioning: an absolute fast on any critical statements for this day."

As I pondered this assignment I realized there was an even humorous side to this kind of fast. What did the Lord want to show me?

For the first half of the day, I simply felt a void, almost as if I had been wiped out as a person. This was especially true at lunch with my husband, Len, my mother, son Jeff and my secretary, Jeanne Sevigny, present. Several topics came up (school prayer, abortion, the ERA amendment) about which I had definite opinions. I listened to the others and kept silent. Barbed comments on the tip of my tongue about certain world leaders were suppressed. In our talkative family no one seemed to notice.

Bemused, I noticed that my comments were not missed. The federal government, the judicial system, and the institutional church could apparently get along fine without my penetrating observations. But still I didn't see what this fast on criticism was accomplishing—until mid-afternoon.

For several years I had been praying for one talented young man whose life had gotten sidetracked. Perhaps my prayers for him had been too negative. That afternoon, a specific, positive vision for this life was dropped into my mind with God's unmistakable hallmark on it—joy.

Ideas began to flow in a way I had not experienced in years. Now it was apparent what the Lord wanted me to see. My critical nature had not corrected a single one of the multitudinous things I found fault with. What it *had* done was to stifle my own creativity—in prayer, in relationships, perhaps even in writing—ideas that He wanted to give me.

Last Sunday night in a Bible study group, I told of my Day's Fast experiment. The response was startling. Many admitted that criticalness was the chief problem in their offices, or in their marriages, or with their teenage children.

My own character flaw here is not going to be corrected overnight. But in thinking this problem through the past few days, I find the most solid scriptural basis possible for dealing with it. (The Greek word translated "judge" in King James, becomes "criticize" in Moffatt.) All through the Sermon on the Mount, Jesus sets Himself squarely against our seeing other people and life situations through this negative lens.

What He is showing me so far can be summed up as follows:

1)   A critical spirit focuses us on ourselves and makes us unhappy. We lose perspective and humor.

2)   A critical spirit blocks the positive creative thoughts God longs to give us.

3)   A critical spirit can prevent good relationships between individuals and often produces retaliatory criticalness.

4)   Criticalness blocks the work of the Spirit of God: love, good will, mercy.

5)   Whenever we see something genuinely wrong in another person's behavior, rather than criticize him or her directly, or—far worse—gripe about him behind his back, we should ask the Spirit of God to do the correction needed.

Convicted of the true destructiveness of a critical mind-set, on my knees I am repeating this prayer: "Lord, I repent of this sin of judgment. I am deeply sorry for having committed so gross an offense against You and against myself so continually. I claim Your promise of forgiveness and seek a new beginning."

5

Thou Fool

I visited my friend Virginia Lively in Belle Glade, Florida, on Sunday afternoon. Out of several hours of prayer together came— among other things—the conviction that my relationship with and attitude to B——— needs to be corrected by Jesus, especially in the spiritual realm.

This morning, Lord, You brought to my remembrance Your words, "Whosoever shall say to his brother . . . Thou fool, shall be in danger of hell fire" (Matthew 5:22 KJV).

Well, I have certainly been saying that of B———, and thinking it. How clearly I see this now, Lord, as the sin of spiritual and intellectual pride. So I confess this sin of mental and verbal judgment. I ask You to forgive me for my arrogance and to cleanse me. Bring my attitude toward, my every thought of, my every reaction toward, and my every word about or to B——— in line with Your view of her.

Cleanse me of every holier-than-thou stance. Since I am "hidden in Christ," then my opinion of anyone doesn't matter. Only Jesus' opinion matters.

Thank You, Lord, for Your acceptance of this confession. Thank You for Your forgiveness. Thank You for the beginning right now of a new relationship with B———. Thank You for dealing with her in Your all-seeing love. Thank You for lifting the burden of resentment and judging from me. I *do* feel tons lighter already. Thank You!!

6

Jesus Makes the Decisions

Yesterday I began trying to get back to a real *quiet time* in the early morning. My directive was, "Never mind about reading. Spend the time getting in touch with Jesus directly."

For a couple of days prior to this the Holy Spirit had dropped a curious clause from Scripture into my mind and heart: "And the government shall be upon [Jesus'] shoulder . . ." (Isaiah 9:6 KJV). I had never thought of this in relation to the government of *my* life. Suddenly it spoke volumes to me . . . the responsibility of my life is now His, the burden *He* will carry. He will make the decisions, the right decisions. What a relief: what joy to turn it over to Him.

Yesterday I mostly just asked Him questions, knowing that sooner or later in His time, He will answer them. He well knows my questioning spirit. I don't think He minds that.

Having posed my questions, I left them there, in His hands . . . and felt sweet peace flow into my spirit.

A while ago I was told that I was to refrain from criticism for one month, a fast of the tongue. Now I am directed to extend this curbing of my faultfinding into the thought area.

The Spirit reminded me of Jesus' words, "Sufficient unto the day is the evil thereof." Clearly then, Jesus recognizes the evil all around us in our daily walk. Simply, for the time being, I am not to let my mind dwell there. The Spirit also showed me that the tidiness of my possessions and papers has a direct bearing on my peace on the inside. Rather than let this chore weigh on me as an added pressure, though, I am to let Him direct me *when* to undertake straightening up my things.

7

The Dry Period

I've been off on a familiar barren road recently and need to get down on paper the steps I took to get back on the main highway. I'm talking about the *dry period.* The state is always much the same for me: shriveled and lonely on the inside. I can't do any writing. I'm unable to accomplish much of anything, just going through the motions of life and barely able to do that. Worst of all—shut off from God.

In her book *Mysticism,* Evelyn Underhill points out that such experiences are a necessary part of the Christian walk.

> For those who have trod the Christian way for some time, a spiritual and psychic fatigue occasionally creeps in and overcomes one. In this

state one knows anew the helplessness of us humans. Yet here, for a time, we are in a worse state than at the beginning of our Christian walk. For at that early stage, along with the helplessness, there was the sure and wonderful knowledge of God's adequacy.

Now the skies seem totally deaf; no glorious light breaks through at all. Nothing, inside or outside, seems to work. If one can ride it through on sheer blind faith, just hanging onto the rock of salvation, *then* it has to pass, and we go on into an advanced state in the spiritual life.

The reason this dry state is necessary, she points out, is that we have to find anew our need, become desperate in a new way, in order to get on with the next stage in our Christian development.

We know that physically and emotionally the developing self advances through a series of growth spurts interspersed with pauses on plateaus. Apparently, the same process holds in the spiritual life.

So the way out of this latest dry period for me began with an admission of my helplessness. And not just a grudging acknowledgment, but a trusting and expectant *acceptance*, relying on Jesus' promise that *His* strength is made perfect in *my* weakness (see 2 Corinthians 12:9).

Next, I was not only to bear this dry and barren stretch of life, but actually to *thank* God for it. My praise to Him lacked enthusiasm at first, but as always the Psalms supplied the words I could not. (Psalms 95, 100, 103 are some of my favorites.) Gradually my cup began to fill and my spirit to loosen.

The last step was to show someone I loved them; in this case it was a visit to a bed-bound neighbor.

Before going back to my writing, I asked the Holy Spirit for specific help in setting up the story sequences in my novel. Soon a wonderful thing began to happen. I could feel my creative nature thrusting down its rootlets in search of the life-giving Water at some deep level in my being. Bit by bit, episode by episode, I watched the lineaments of the story line emerging in my mind. It was as if I could see the bulbs I planted in the ground last fall begin their growth in the cold and the dark. Even the creative process that formed the earth, I reflected, began in *darkness*.

It takes acceptance and praise and outgoing love for me to emerge from a dry period, but, oh, the exhilaration that follows!

8

To Forgive . . . and Forget

*T*his morning I had to face up to the fact that I still had a bad attitude toward a woman who is constantly attacking me and my writings. On taking it to the Lord, I received two insights:

(1) The reason I am so upset is that *I haven't forgiven her completely.* I've made stabs at this in the past, but as she comes to my mind I have an almost physical sensation, as of iron bars pressing against my chest. The Lord showed me that on the other side of these bars was a woman, a human being, who needed to be freed. So, on my knees before Him, I went through a process of unreservedly forgiving her by an act of my will. I confessed my feelings about her and asked God to make the forgiveness real.

(2) My job was not finished, however, He told me, until *I can forget what she has done.*

"But *how can* I do that, Lord?"

Your will is greater than your memory, Catherine. Rebuke the painful memory and cast it out in the name of Jesus.

I was to ". . . bring into captivity every thought to the obedience of Christ" (2 Corinthians 10:5 KJV). Then to ask forgiveness for hanging onto these memories (we tend to stab ourselves again and again with old, hurtful episodes), and ask for an alarm system on the door of my mind whenever the memory tries to creep back.

From henceforth I am to look at this woman—*and at anyone else who has ever hurt me*—with eyes of compassion and love, concentrating on the potential they have for good. Only thus will I be able to see them as Jesus does.

"But Lord . . . will this approach bring about changes in them?"

That's between them and Me. You will have peace.

9

The Key to Obedience

Am struggling this morning with the seeming contradiction between Jesus' constant stress on *obedience* as crucial to Christian growth,
over against the reality of "grace," which is the "unmerited favor of
God."

Obedience would seem to be our going up the ladder step by step,
not earning our way exactly, while continually dependent on still
putting forth our own efforts. Whereas the teaching all through the
Bible is that it is God who always takes the initiative with us. All of
God's good gifts are given by pure grace; there is no way we can
deserve a single one of them.

So—exactly where and how does obedience fit into this?

I'm beginning to see that the missing key here is Love. The chief characteristic of love is wanting to do what pleases the beloved. The analogy Jesus used most often was filial love: He meant His relationship to His Father to be the pattern for *our* relationship to Him (Jesus). Jesus' obedience was not the result of gritted teeth and grim determination, but the natural outworking of love: "I do as the Father has commanded me, so that the world may know (be convinced) that I love the Father . . ." (John 14:31 AMPLIFIED).

When we truly love someone, our focus is on *him* or *her,* not on ourselves. And our constant thought is, "What can I do to give this beloved person joy? To please him? To ease his path? To minister to him?"

It staggers my mind to think that I can in any way minister to Jesus, or gladden His heart. Yet this is the gracious message of the Gospel, which always puts the emphasis on love:

"We love Him, because He first loved us" (1 John 4:19 AMPLIFIED).

God's grace, God's initiative.

". . . If a person [really] loves Me, he will keep My word—obey My teaching" (John 14:23 AMPLIFIED).

Our natural, unforced response.

10

Worry:
Be Gone

*T*his morning I awoke full of worry about the future, with Len having resigned from his job as editor of *Guideposts*. Len and I were in agreement about this step, and he is enthusiastic about going into book publishing with John and Elizabeth Sherrill, but I see so many obstacles ahead, especially when his salary check stops coming.

Then the Lord directed me to the fourth chapter of Philippians, particularly to verse 8 (AMPLIFIED, italics added):

> . . . whatever is worthy of reverence . . .
> is honorable and seemly . . .

is just . . .
is pure . . .
is lovely and lovable . . .
is kind and winsome and gracious,
if there is any
virtue . . .
excellence . . .
anything worthy of praise,
[we are to] think on
and weigh
and take account of these things—
fix your minds on them.

Now this might seem to be the worst kind of not facing reality were it not for the fact that earlier in the same chapter Paul has already exhorted us (v. 6) to pray about *everything,* to pour our hearts out to the Heavenly Father with "definite requests."

My problem is that having done this, having laid my concern before the Father, I get the feeling that if I do not frequently return to it in my mind and keep "worrying" it, much as a dog would a bone, then there certainly can be no chance of solving it. It's a feeling that it would actually be irresponsible or frivolous *not* to do this—wrong to think about other things, and go my merry way while a major problem faces us.

I slip into the worry stance in spite of telling myself over and over that God is the problem-solver, that we can confidently leave our situation in His hands. I know what I should do, yet emotionally and practically I do not act out this letting go. This morning God seems to be pointing out chapter four in Philippians as a blueprint for handling crises His way:

1) Regardless of any circumstances, we are to *rejoice in the Lord always.*
2) We are *not* to fret or have anxiety about *anything.*
3) We are to pray about everything, making our needs and wants known unto God.

4) We are to be content with our earthly lot, whatever it is.

5) We are to guard our thoughts, think only upon upbeat, positive things—nothing negative. If we will do the above, then we are promised:

   a) God's peace . . . shall garrison and mount guard over our hearts and minds in Christ Jesus.

   b) Christ will "infuse inner strength into us"— that is, "We will be self-sufficient in Christ's sufficiency."

LL Note: God honored our leap of faith into book publishing. Chosen Books, from its inception, produced books that made a major impact on both the Christian and secular world.

11

His Peace

*T*his morning the Lord asked me to look up the Scripture verse "the things that belong unto thy peace." With the help of a concordance, I found it in Luke 19:41–42 KJV. The scene is a hill overlooking Jerusalem.

> . . . [Jesus] beheld the city, and wept over it, Saying If thou hadst known, even thou, at least in this thy day, the things which belong unto thy peace! but now they are hid from thine eyes.

Lord, what do You want me to understand from this? What are the things that belong to my peace?

Surely, this ties in with the "rest" that was the other message given me this morning.

There remaineth, therefore, a rest to the people of God. For he that
is entered into his rest, he also hath ceased from his own works. . . .

Hebrews 4:9–10 KJV

In the midst of disquiet about so many things in our life right
now—my trying to make progress on my novel, the Chosen Books
situation in general, my declining eyesight due to cataracts, poor
sleep, etc., the message Jesus wants me to have today seems to be
simply, "Peace! Rest in Me. I am here to give you, Catherine, the
precious gift of peace of mind and spirit."

How glorious! He confirms it in Scripture after Scripture (italics
added):

May grace (God's favor) and *peace* (which is perfect well-being, all
necessary good, all spiritual prosperity and freedom from fears and
agitating passions and moral conflicts), be multiplied to you. . . .

2 Peter 1:2 AMPLIFIED

For though the mountains should depart and the hills be shaken or
removed, yet My love and kindness shall not depart from you, nor
shall My covenant of peace and completeness be removed, says the
Lord, Who has compassion on you.

Isaiah 54:10 AMPLIFIED

Praise You, Lord Jesus! Praise You!!

The next day . . .

I discovered yesterday that the beautiful freedom the Lord gave me
in His gracious promises of "peace" carried along with it the joy of a
moment-by-moment obedience.

That is, during the day I made the discovery that I had departed
from the habit of looking directly to Jesus for the answer to small daily
decisions; that the only way I will keep a pliable, obedient spirit in the
larger decisions, is to look to Him and *to obey* in the smaller ones.

I had slipped badly on that. I'm always getting hung up on the
tension, or seeming tension, between freedom in Christ Jesus and
obedience.

James, however, makes this connection beautifully:

> But the man who looks intently into the perfect law that gives
> freedom, and continues to do this, not forgetting what he has heard,
> but doing it—he will be blessed in what he does.
>
> James 1:25 NIV

Or to approach all this another way. I see that Satan has small
chance of getting at us—of accusing us and destroying our rest (as he
has with me so often over "small" things like sleeping pills, or the
lipstick issue I faced years ago on Cape Cod) when we are faithful in
present-moment obedience, steadily looking to Jesus, asking, "Shall I
do this? Or not?"—and then obeying.

Thus this obedience *results* in liberty—and the two go hand in hand.

12

Idolatry

A couple of days ago Len and I had a heated discussion about the subject matter for the Tuesday evening Bible class and how we were going to teach it. He did not accept—or even understand—what I was saying, and it annoyed me that I could not get my point across.

That night I had a dream in which I was pursued by photographers. Flattered, I allowed them to take a series of pictures. When they appeared in print, I was horrified. The photos were obnoxious, nasty, almost obscene. To my eyes, the pictures clearly said, "She's a big show-off."

Through the dream I believe God was revealing to me my arrogance and self-righteousness about my *opinions*. I saw that this has always been one of my problems with the children, Linda especially. "Love me, love my opinions!" Ideas are very, very important to me, and I consider *my* ideas uncommonly valuable.

How ironic that the very passage over which Len and I disagreed— the giving of the Law to Moses—included as the first Commandment of all: *Thou shalt have no other gods before me* (Exodus 20:3 KJV).

Before bedtime that night I confessed to God and to Len my idolatry of my own passionately held convictions.

13

Self-denial _____

*L*ast night at bedtime I ate several pieces of candy, which was wrong from every point of view: pure gratification of self's momentary desire.

This morning I could not worship the Lord. Something was coming between us. Then the Spirit spoke gently, *"Deny yourself* . . . pick up your cross daily and follow Me." It was as if He were putting His finger on the words "Deny yourself." I had never noticed them particularly in that passage. I wasn't even certain those two words were there. So I looked up the verse; they were there all right. I also got illumination on the rest of the passage: "For whoever wants to save his [higher, spiritual, eternal] life, will lose [the lower, natural, temporal life which is lived (only) on earth]" (Mark 8:35 AMPLIFIED).

I saw that Jesus is here simply stating a fact of life. If I want to lose weight, I must give up the lower desire for stuffing my mouth in order to attain the higher desire of a fit, healthy body.

If I want to write a book, I must give up the use of my time for other things.

For the first time I glimpse the rationale of certain spiritual exercises, such as fasting.

Lord, teach me!

14

Self-denial: The Teaching Goes On

*A*n insight today on how to make the denial of some small pleasure not only less painful but even an almost joyous event.

Up to this point in my life, whenever I've thought I was hearing the Lord's voice telling me to give up something that I loved, I could—and often would—drag my feet for weeks and months. Often I've had to pray the laggard's prayer, "O Lord, make me willing to be made willing." Almost always I've thought of obedience to the Lord as really quite painful.

But now after so many years of my Christian walk, a change is taking place within me. Jesus is becoming much more real to me as a person. I believe that what has been happening to me recently is the beginning of the direct fulfillment of this passage (italics added):

> The person who has My commands and keeps them is the one who [really] loves Me, and whoever [really] loves Me will be loved by My Father. And I [too] will love him and *will show* (reveal, manifest) *Myself to him—I will let Myself be clearly seen by him and make Myself real to him.*
>
> John 14:21 AMPLIFIED

For quite a stretch I've been getting the message that Jesus was displeased with my 5:00 to 6:00 P.M. "Happy Hour," a time for relaxed reading or listening to music, when I sip a glass of sherry. At first I thought He wanted me to give up the sherry. Lately I've seen that it isn't so much what He wants me to give up, but that He wants me to be active physically during this hour, to walk or work in the garden. I had let myself become too lazy and sedentary, and too rigid about this 5:00 to 6:00 P.M. pattern. *I* like my ruts. *He* wants me active, and above all, flexible.

Then He began teaching me about *how* He goes about changing long-standing habits. It's part of the outworking of the great promise,

> This is the covenant which I will make with the house of Israel after those days, says the Lord: I will put my law . . . upon their hearts; and I will be their God, and they shall be my people.
>
> Jeremiah 31:33 RSV

I had never before tied this promise to the problems connected with habit changing. I have no addiction to alcohol or smoking, or sweets, for instance, but I ache for certain persons I know who do. I see now how He helps us with these ingrained patterns when we ask Him for help. What happens is that *our* tastes begin to change. Something that we liked a lot suddenly is not so appealing. When we understand *how* He works and that this *is* the Lord Himself working, then we can stop resisting our own changing tastes, thank Him, and flow with the new direction of the tide.

It's a marvelous plan only He could have thought of, for there is no pain in ceasing to do what we no longer care to do.

15

The Temptation of Things

I've been through a small siege of temptation to worldliness that I'm almost embarrassed to write about—and yet feel I should.

From the time I was a small girl I've loved pretty, feminine things, especially jewelry. Nothing very unusual or terribly wrong about that. For most of my life I could not afford jewelry, so it was no issue.

Even when in recent years I could afford some jewelry, the Depression syndrome that permeated my family for many years has kept me frugal. One day a check for several hundred dollars arrived that I hadn't expected. "Now I can get those gold earrings," I said to myself.

So I began making trips to jewelry stores looking for the exactly right earrings. Then an inner restlessness began to ruffle me. So I started to argue with God.

"Lord, are You telling me that earrings are too frivolous?"

Silence.

"It isn't as though I'm buying them from my tithe funds. I mean, the money is extra. I hadn't expected it."

Silence.

"Lord, I've spent much more for a rug or a piece of furniture without this guilt complex. Now, really, isn't this inner disquiet just my Puritan, Depression-born complex?"

Then came the gentle response:

I'm concerned over the inordinate amount of time you've given to this in your thought life.

At once I was led to the apostle John's comment on worldliness and his warning about the "delight of the eyes":

> Do not love or cherish the world or the things that are in the world. If any one loves the world, love for the Father is not in him.
>
> For all that is in the world, the lust of the flesh [craving for sensual gratification], and the lust of the eyes [greedy longings of the mind] and the pride of life [assurance in one's own resources or in the stability of earthly things]—these do not come from the Father but from the world [itself].
>
> And the world passes away and disappears. . . .
>
> 1 John 2:15–17 AMPLIFIED

Here John is taking us into the higher reaches of spirituality. He doesn't use the word "sin"; he doesn't mention Satan. He's concerned with whether we realize the extent of God's love for us—and how much love for God there is in us.

The crux of it: the love exchange between God and me is going to suffer if I focus too much on worldly things.

16

Fear of Man

The Lord is having me look at something this morning that is very unsettling. It came first through the following verse:

> The fear of man bringeth a snare: but whoso putteth his trust in the Lord shall be safe.
>
> Proverbs 29:25 KJV

I don't fear man in a physical way, but do I fear his disapproval of me? In other words, how much do I try to please other people instead of looking to God alone for His approval? Certainly, there is enormous pressure on all of us to be accepted and approved by others. But God wants us to resist this pressure. Consider the tragedy of the religious leaders of Jesus' day:

> Among the chief rulers also many believed on him; but because of
> the Pharisees they did not confess him, lest they should be put out
> of the synagogue: For they loved the praise of men more than the
> praise of God.
>
> John 12:42–43 KJV

Even Peter, soon to be leader of the earliest church, denied knowing
Jesus at all following His arrest, simply to remain in the good graces
of a motley crowd gathered around a bonfire. Peter was no coward.
When the soldiers had come to seize Jesus, he had grabbed a sword
and cut off the ear of one of them. So it wasn't his life Peter feared for
here, but the ridicule and judgment and opinions of others.

We are told that in our daily task—whatever our vocation or
profession or daily round—we are to seek to please God more than
man:

> Servants, obey in all things your masters according to the flesh; not
> with eyeservice, as menpleasers; but in singleness of heart, fearing
> God.
>
> Colossians 3:22 KJV

The thought comes that my tendency to be critical of others springs
out of the soil of what-people-will-think. What we are, we see in
others. I am judgmental, therefore I expect others to be the same.

Jesus was simply stating a law of life when He told us, ". . . judge
[and] ye shall be judged: and with what measure ye mete, it shall be
measured to you" (Matthew 7:2 KJV). Put this way, judging others
constantly cultivates more soil for the thistles of fear-of-man to grow
in.

Judgmentalism is an attempt to ward off this fear by standing in a
superior place. Self thinks that when it can get there first and judge
before others can state their opinions, it can forestall others' criticisms.
Of course, self is mistaken, since the very opposite happens—judging
draws the judgment of others.

Two passages of Scripture, personalized for this specific fear, are
helping me overcome my exaggerated concern for man's approval:

Fear not [the opinions of others]: for I have redeemed thee; I have called thee by thy name; thou art mine.

Isaiah 43:1 KJV

When thou passest through the waters [of ridicule], I will be with thee; and through the rivers [of rejection], they shall not overflow thee: when thou walkest through the fire [of contempt], thou shalt not be burned; neither shall the flame kindle upon thee.

Isaiah 43:2 KJV

17

Immersed in a Horse Trough

I want to get down in my journal the fascinating experience Len and I had this past weekend. At the urging of our friend Virginia Lively we drove to Clewiston, Florida, about sixty miles from our home here in Boynton Beach. Virginia had gone through what she called a "believer's baptism" in the Episcopal church there. She described it as "a beautiful, cleansing, and healing experience" and urged us to consider doing it.

For months now I have read with fascination about the Jesus people, a California phenomenon. Most seem to be young, former members of the drug culture, who, after a "believer's baptism" in the Pacific Ocean, experience an almost total change of lifestyle.

Virginia's conviction was that every Christian should have the opportunity of undergoing baptism *following* his or her personal decision for Christ. She had been baptized as a very young child in her own Episcopal church and had accepted this sacrament as valid, but she believes that, ideally, we should be "dedicated" to God as babies, then have a "water baptism" later when we are ready to accept Jesus on our own.

I spent a morning digging out Scripture references to baptism, coming on one archetype I'd never noticed:

> For Christ . . . was put to death in the body but made alive by the Spirit, through whom also he went and preached to the spirits in prison who disobeyed long ago when God waited patiently in the days of Noah while the ark was being built. In it only a few people, eight in all, were saved through water, and this water symbolizes baptism that now saves you also—not the removal of dirt from the body but the pledge of a good conscience toward God. . . .
>
> 1 Peter 3:18–21 NIV

Since the subject of baptism has always divided Christians, at first Len and I felt a certain wariness about accepting Virginia's invitation. Then John and Elizabeth (Tib) Sherrill (our close friends and associates at *Guideposts* magazine) arrived for a visit and expressed interest. All four of us had been baptized as infants, long before we could remember. We were convinced that the performance of this sacrament on our behalfs had been complete and theologically adequate in every way. We all agreed, however, that we didn't want to miss anything that the Lord might have for us right now. The Sherrills, LeSourds, my friend Freddie Koch, and her daughter Claudia drove from our home in Boynton Beach last Saturday for a spiritual adventure. In Clewiston we located the home of the Episcopal rector. Virginia Lively had arrived there a few minutes earlier.

The first thing that happened was between John Sherrill and me. Our relationship had become strained through some theological differences. While we sat together in the rector's living room, John began speaking about his fear of change. Twice when there had been major upheavals in his life he had developed cancer. He confessed apprehension of a recurrence in the face of upcoming changes in his and Tib's situation.

At Virginia's urging, he recollected his childhood and talked about the little-boy John—skinny, non-athletic, not popular with the "in" crowd—and tears filled my eyes. How I identified with him there. A new love for John filled me and I went over and hugged him. The reconciliation was complete and almost instantaneous.

Next we went to the nearby Episcopal church, a small sanctuary set in a grove of Florida pine trees. In the vestibule of the church had been placed a galvanized iron horse trough, the stickers from the feed store still visible on one end. A hose, connected to a water spigot outside, ran through the open screen door and was filling the trough. This was to be the setting for the baptism.

First, we sat down in the sanctuary and sang some appropriate hymns. The Episcopal priest, in slacks and sports shirt, prayed, then explained the significance of a believer's baptism: that it was not necessary for salvation, but an opportunity for confession, asking and receiving forgiveness, then making a new commitment of our lives to Jesus. This would open us to a fresh infusion of the Holy Spirit with the resulting new love and joy and power that comes when Jesus indwells us.

As we changed into bathing suits, each of us pondered the areas in our lives where confession and forgiveness were needed. This was done quietly with God, with our spouses, or openly with the rector. The Sherrills led the way, first Tib, then John being immersed.

Afterwards John said softly to Tibby, "Now that we have left our old persons at the bottom of the horse trough and are new creatures, don't you think we ought to get married again?"

The two of them, barefoot, water dripping from their hair and bathing suits, stood before the altar, pledging themselves to one another again. Len and I followed . . . into the horse trough and then to the altar for a reaffirmation of our marriage vows, our eyes brimming with tears.

The next morning, after we got home, we found just outside our front door an elaborate "Just Married" sign which Claudia Koch—who had been wide-eyed during the ceremonies—had made and sometime during the night left at our door.

Section Four _____
His Strength
in Our Weakness _____

At one point during our courtship, Catherine voiced a concern over her health, saying she doubted that she had more than five years to live. I "pooh-poohed" this, pointing to her own mother's robust health at age sixty-seven.

Both of us were wrong. Catherine lived twenty-three years more, but her death at sixty-nine was far short of her mother's life span (Mother Wood is now ninety-four).

And for all of those twenty-three years Catherine battled a debilitating emphysema that sapped her energy and sometimes left her gasping for breath after even so simple an exertion as climbing a flight of stairs. New York winters brought on severe bronchitis. Our move to Boynton Beach, Florida, doubtless prolonged her life, but it did not solve her health problems. Along the way she won a battle over sleeping pills—until her last years when sleeplessness once more turned her nights into a spiritual battleground.

Prayers for Catherine's healing throughout our marriage lifted her, strengthened her, but never totally healed her. "Why?" she asked over and over. The enigma of why some are healed, some are not, frustrated Catherine all her life.

But she never stopped struggling for answers. And out of the struggle came—not the robust health she yearned for, but a daily, growing intimacy with God that became far more precious than any amount of physical stamina. Her constant companion on this closer walk . . . the Bible.

LL

I

Trusting God

Today this verse in Psalm 37 spoke to me:

> Commit your way to the Lord—roll and repose [each care of] your load on Him; trust (lean on, rely on and be confident) also in Him, and He will bring it to pass.
>
> Psalm 37:5 AMPLIFIED

This is my husband Len's favorite verse of the entire Bible. He has leaned on this passage in recent years while making the switch from editing a magazine to publishing Christian books.

There is much in Scripture stressing our need to have faith in God. The above verse takes us a step further. It not only admonishes us to trust, it promises that when we do, God will act in a supernatural way to answer our need. Dwell on that for a moment. We trust, God acts. A mind-blowing premise.

Yet total, all-out trust on our part is not as easy as it first seems. There are periods when God's face is shrouded, when His dealings with us will *appear* as if He does not care, when He seems not to be acting like a true Father. Can we then hang onto the fact of His love and His faithfulness and that He *is* a prayer-answering God?

Can we get to the point Habakkuk reached: "Though the fig tree does not blossom, and there be no fruit on the vines . . . Yet I will rejoice in the Lord . . . !" (Habakkuk 3:17–18 AMPLIFIED).

Can we, *at the moment* when His face is hidden, exult in the God of our salvation? "The Lord God is my strength, my personal bravery and my invincible army" (v. 19).

Last Saturday morning Len had a chance to demonstrate the principle of trust in a difficult situation. He awoke with a very bad throat condition; could hardly speak. Yet he was supposed to give a talk that morning at a men's prayer breakfast in the local Lutheran church.

Before he left for the church I anointed him with oil, placed my hand on his throat, and asked the Lord to do a healing work in Len for the glory of God.

During the breakfast preceding Len's speech, however, he told me later, his voice got worse and worse until there was little left but a croak. The Lutheran pastor suggested turning the gathering into a discussion group, giving Len the chance to bow out. But no, my husband would at least try.

So Len stood up and uttered a rasping, halting first sentence, literally plunging ahead on faith. Suddenly, he reported afterwards, his voice cleared. From then on, for thirty-odd minutes, the message poured out with no cough, hardly even a clearing of the throat. The Holy Spirit had simply taken over. In the question period afterwards, still no problem with his throat.

But when he returned home, Len's voice was once again a painful whisper.

What fascinated me in this episode is how biblical it is: as the symptoms get worse, the temptation is there to "give up" and not to trust Jesus. We must resist that temptation in the midst of our very real human helplessness, "roll" the entire burden onto His shoulders, as He bade us do, step out and *take the first step* with bare, no-evidence-at-all, faith.

And lo, He does take over gloriously, doing what we literally cannot do for ourselves.

2

Lord, I Resent . . . _____

Thank [God] in everything—no matter what the circumstances may
be, be thankful and give thanks; for this is the will of God for you
[who are] in Christ Jesus. . . .

1 Thessalonians 5:18 AMPLIFIED

Yesterday morning in my prayer time, God showed me that if I
wanted more vitality for my work hours, I had to deal with the
following resentments that were smoldering inside me.

I resent my lack of social graces in certain situations, which I'm
inclined to blame on my childhood years when I too often fled social
encounters.

I resent the fact that I'm such a poor sleeper. I can see that resentment produces tension and, of course, accumulated tension through the day is one reason I'm not sleeping better.

Here at Evergreen Farm there are so many stairs to climb, and outside, hills and more hills, which I cannot mount because of my breathlessness. This condition is a constant embarrassment and the central thorn in my flesh. I resent my damaged lungs.

I see this morning that there are deeper resentments still: that of creeping old age, being progressively shut down, as it were, and, of course, out there—death. Have I not always resented the fact of death, even though I have total belief in and expectancy about the life after death?

How can I come to terms with all this?

The answer came in the above verse. I am to praise God for *all* things, regardless of where they seem to originate. Doing this, He points out, is the key to receiving the blessings of God. Praise will wash away my resentments. I've known this, accepted it, even written about praise. But as I began praising Him yesterday, my efforts were wooden.

Then came these thoughts: I was to ignore my feelings and act on the principle. I was to do it despite the lack of joy—simply because God told me to. True praise grows out of the recognition and acknowledgment that in His time God will bring good out of bad. There is the intolerable situation on the one hand and the fulfillment of Romans 8:28 on the other hand. ("All things work together for good. . . .") By an act of will and through imagination and with faith, I am to turn my back on the bad and face the good, and begin actively to praise God for it as Scripture commands.

Shortly after this insight, my cleaning woman called in to say that she was not coming. Praised God for this, though mechanically.

Following that, joy began spilling over into the tiny everydayness of my life. Walked by a vase of beautiful roses from our garden and buried my nose in the fragrance, saying, "Praise You, Lord, for such beauty!"

Stepped onto our patio for a moment to listen to the birds singing. "Praise You, Lord, for all Your creatures."

Then came the feeling that all these small acts put together—little trickles of praise—were running together, beginning to form a river of praise.

Continued to praise God for *all* things, good and bad. All setbacks, frustrations, and resentments.

Praise You, Lord, for my awkwardness in certain social situations.

Praise You, Lord, that I have trouble sleeping.

Praise You, Lord, for my weak lungs.

Praise You, Lord, for creeping old age.

Praise You, Lord, for the death that comes to all of us.

This morning I actually woke up with praise swelling in my heart. Only later did I realize I had slept through the entire night! Cannot remember when I last did this! Awakened by the coffee pot going on. Imagine! Praise God indeed!

3

Do I Really Want to Get Well?

My heart is heavy this morning as I think of Rosalind. She is almost bedridden now with asthma. We went to pray for her healing yesterday, but she was more interested in talking about her ailments than in receiving Christ's love and power. How tragic!

This morning I turned again to the Gospel of John for the story of the man at the Pool of Bethesda who had been ill for thirty-eight years. As I read, I pretended I was there in Jerusalem myself, watching in the shadow of one of those great arched colonnades around the long pool. I could shut my eyes and see the scene as if it were happening today.

The man in this account is a chronic invalid, probably in his fifties or sixties. The stone floor around the large pool is crowded with the pallets of the crippled and the blind. But this man has been there longer than any. He is now the old-timer; his illness has virtually become his career and status symbol.

Now Jesus appears, threading His way through the porticos. He looks into the eyes of the sick man: "Do you want to become well?" (John 5:6 AMPLIFIED).

It seems a ridiculous question on the surface. Wouldn't anyone want to be healed of a physical handicap? But surprisingly the invalid begins to stammer excuses.

"Sir," he replies to Jesus, "it's just that I haven't anybody to put me into the pool when the angel of healing is present. While I'm trying to get there, somebody else always gets into the water first."

As I read these words I knew that this sick man's problem was Rosalind's problem too. He thought he wanted healing, but even to his own ears his rationalizations must sound hollow. Yet those amazing eyes boring into his hold no contempt. Rather, Jesus issues a loving directive in a voice that rings with authority. "Pick up your bed and walk."

This is the moment of truth. I could picture the emotions moving across the pinched features: surprise, consternation, doubt, awareness, hope, then resolution. The man scrambles to his feet, picks up his bedroll, a well man.

How much this story says to me every time I read it—and can say to anyone who finds his fervent petitions unanswered. The principle here is: True prayer is dominant desire. If the person is divided in his real yearnings, he will experience emptiness and frustration.

I still remember vividly the three years in the 1940s when I myself was bedridden. Little by little I had come to enjoy my quiet life. I thought that I yearned for healing, but in fact I was not ready to shoulder the full responsibilities of vigorous health.

Only when I asked the Lord to mend my inner confusion was I able to go all-out in prayer. The healing of my physical disability followed.

Since that experience, I have been able to perceive this divided self as a major stumbling block to many people. I think of my friend in Washington, Jessie, who had been praying long and hard for her husband to be healed of alcoholism. Jessie was spiritually minded, her husband worldly and cynical. He was contemptuous of his wife's frequent trips to retreats and church meetings.

Several of us met regularly to pray with Jessie that her husband would encounter the living Christ for himself. Thanks to a group of vital Christian men, this came about, gloriously. John became a re-covered alcoholic and a changed man.

The surprise was Jessie's reaction. Her criticism of John continued unabated. For the first time we, her friends, suspected the divided will in Jessie. Our suspicions were confirmed one night when one of the women suggested that Jessie thank God for so great an answer to our prayers for John.

Jessie could not do it. The words would not come. Then we understood. For years Jessie's prayers for John had gone unanswered because she had enjoyed standing above John on her pedestal marked "spiritual." Admired by friends for her suffering and patience with an alcoholic husband, she came to enjoy her martyr role. Therefore, the unsuspected desire of her deepest being had canceled out the prayer of her lips for John's conversion. Only when she was able to see this divided self and surrender it to God was she able to work out a better relationship with her husband.

It is so clear to me this morning. The divided self can defeat us in every area. Like finding the right job. When we hear the job-seeker insist on a string of specific conditions regarding salary, hours, pension, geographic location—we will often find a cleavage in his aspirations.

Fortunately, there is something we can do about the contradictions inside us.

First, we can present our long-standing, unanswered prayers to God for analysis. If there is any division of will deep inside, He will put His finger on it. This will hurt. We will be shocked—even as the man at the pool was, even as Jessie was.

Second, we can acknowledge this inner inconsistency and present it,

without cringing or making excuses, to God for healing, asking Him
to bring our conscious and subconscious minds into harmony. At this
point He will almost always issue us a directive as Jesus did the man
at the poolside. He asks that we prove our wholeheartedness by obedience. The moment that we rise to obey Him, we discover a great
fact: that the word of God and the work of God are one. His words *are*
life—with power to restore the atrophied will, to quicken pallid desire, to resurrect us from the graveclothes of a half-dead existence.

4

To Live
in the Present Moment

I want to record this morning that I did something yesterday, November 5, 1978, I do too seldom. For a period of time I lived fully in the present moment. What a healing this was for my spirit.

It happened in church. Six members of our family were sitting in the same pew.

Beside me was my tall son Peter, then his beautiful wife, Edith, and their two children, Mary Elizabeth and Peter Jonathan; on my other side, Len—so faithful, so solid. And we were all healthy and together and of one mind in the Lord. Great surges of gratitude washed over me and I was happier than I have been in a long time.

The Spirit seemed to say, "Bask in the moment. No matter that the future may hold problems. This is yours."

I did bask. It was golden.

My thankfulness flowed beyond the church walls. I thanked Him for my mother—now eighty-seven—who is still with us with her serene, cheerful disposition. How blessed I am, Lord, to have had You choose such a woman to bear me! I thank You for her lifelong gentleness . . . her womanliness, her unwavering faithfulness, her vision that always could lift our dreams on wings and send them flying beyond drudgery or mundane circumstances.

And for Len's three children, grown now, all Christians, each on the right path to his or her own fulfillment. How grateful I am for what they have taught me.

At that beautiful moment God seemed to be shining a light on each member of my family, saying, "See what I have wrought. Enjoy them, be thankful for them, for everything I make is good."

And my response this morning is to thank Him and praise Him in these words I find in His book:

> Give thanks to the Lord, for he is good; his love endures forever.
>
> Psalm 107:1 NIV

> O Lord my God, you are very great; you are clothed with splendor and majesty.
>
> Psalm 104:1 NIV

> Shout for joy to the Lord, all the earth. Worship the Lord with gladness; come before him with joyful songs. . . . Enter his gates with thanksgiving and his courts with praise; give thanks to him and praise his name.
>
> Psalm 100:1–2, 4 NIV

> Thanks be to God! He gives us the victory through our Lord Jesus Christ.
>
> 1 Corinthians 15:57 NIV

5

Helplessness

When I was still not asleep last night about 1:00 A.M., I swallowed one mild sleeping pill. No sleep! At five minutes to three, feeling empty, I got up, went to the kitchen, ate two Ritz crackers with peanut butter, drank a paper cup full of milk, and went back to bed.

Still no sleep! About 4:00 A.M., I took a second sleeping pill. It had no effect at all. I saw dawn break and finally got up.

I got down on my knees and prayed something like, "Lord, You have promised to talk to Your friends. Would you tell me what this is all about?"

I drank a cup of coffee in bed, had my quiet time—Bible reading, etc. No answer from Him. Dead silence.

Got down on my knees again and prayed. No response.

Or . . . was I simply not listening to the message He was speaking? As I was dressing, light began to dawn: He wants to demonstrate to me that I really am helpless without Him, that I really am dependent on Him *even for the sleeping pills to work*. Jesus put it this way:

> Apart from Me—cut off from vital union with Me—you can do nothing.
>
> John 15:5 AMPLIFIED

Since I am stubborn, He has been forced to bring this oh, so-very-basic truth home to me the hard way.

It was on the subject of sleep—the subject *I* wanted to know about—that He was silent. He did not promise me a thing, not that I would sleep beautifully without the sleeping pills, nor that I would sleep *with* them, this afternoon or tonight; nothing. Apparently, He wants me to place this whole area trustingly into His hands, believing that He loves me and wants me to be full of the vitality that comes from adequate sleep. Total dependence, that's the all-important lesson He wants me to learn. For regardless of what I do or do not do, whether I'm in a period of trusting Him or of pulling away, *He* never forgets that I belong to Him, that my life has been paid for with a price. *He* never lets me go!

This is such a *tremendous* base fact to know and to build on and to lean on.

Praise God for this tough experience!

6

Spiritual Preparation
for Surgery

*T*his morning I can look back over the past weeks and see so clearly how God works in adversity. It began over a month ago with the doctor's words, "You're going to need surgery. . . ."

The procedure was "routine," he assured me, the problem most likely "minor," but no casual approach could soften the impact of the next sentence: "Of course, we never know what we'll find." Statistics on cancer then followed. "With this type of ovarian cyst, the percentage of malignancy is . . ."

Thus began a month's battle with fear. As I drove home from the doctor's office that beautiful September afternoon, the brilliant color of the autumn leaves seemed tarnished. How is it, I marveled, that bad news has a way of invading human life so suddenly? Trouble rings no warning bells. Adversity and sorrow stalk into life on rubber soles.

"Fear is lack of faith," I told myself. "It dishonors God." But then I discovered that I could not handle fear any more than I could mastermind any other strong emotion.

As Len and I talked over my situation, our first reaction was the very human one: "Is this operation really necessary?" However "routine" such surgery might be for the doctor, my inadequate lungs make any use of anesthesia a questionable risk. On the medical level, a second opinion seemed the wise course. We pursued this; the second examination confirmed the first.

Next came our conviction that we needed to pose the same question in prayer: "Lord, what is Your will? Do You want to handle my case through prayer alone?"

After all, Scripture provides clear directives and means of grace, which we ignore to our own detriment. From James 5:13–15: prayer with a group of fellow Christians, followed by the laying on of hands and/or anointing with oil by church elders or spiritual leaders. From I Corinthians 11:23–30: prayer at the altar rail of a church by a priest or pastor, with the laying on of hands and/or Communion.

How wonderful it is when God wants to move in this direct manner, and the way is clear for Him to do so! This is what happened to John Sherrill back in 1960 when a suspicious lump was discovered in John's neck and an operation scheduled to remove it. Since a melanoma cancer had been surgically removed from his ear two years before, John asked his rector for the ancient laying-on-of-hands ministry of the Episcopal Church.

Twenty-four hours later, when the famous cancer specialist at New York's Memorial Hospital operated, all he could find was a tiny, dried-up nodule. No lump, no malignancy. I know of other instances equally dramatic, where God has chosen to heal without medical intervention.

In my case, a group of fellow Christians began to meet with Len and me for prayer at 7:30 each morning. My crisis was their crisis. After two weeks in which we sought God's healing, I went for still one more examination. The doctor found no change. More intensive prayer followed; with it came the assurance that I was to go ahead with the operation, that my lungs would withstand the strain, and that there would be no cancer.

Apparently this was one of those times when God wishes us to make use of the skilled hands of surgeons. (God may have other purposes too, of course, such as some personal contact in the hospital He wishes us to make for Him.)

The next step in preparation came over the long-distance telephone from a Christian physician in North Carolina. "Over several years," he told me, "I have seen an incredible difference in the patient's post-operative condition between those who saturate surgery with prayer and those who don't. Most anyone facing surgery has fears. We can't just will them away. But God can handle our fears.

"Another thing," he went on. "Those undergirded with prayer often escape sticky little complications and just sail through the recovery. They even heal faster."

What helped me most of all during those long hours the night before the operation were two Scripture verses. The first promise spoke to fear:

> Fear not; [there is nothing to fear]. . . . For I, the Lord your God, hold your right hand; I, Who say to you, Fear not, I will help you!
> Isaiah 41:10, 13 AMPLIFIED

The second Scripture was a promise from the Psalms:

> Though I walk in the midst of trouble, thou wilt revive me . . . thy right hand shall save me.
> Psalm 138:7 KJV

As I read these reassuring words, a clear picture was dropped into my mind, childlike in its simplicity: the Lord would be standing on the right side of the operating table, facing me, looking into my eyes.

Of course. He would have to be in that position since the Isaiah promise was that He would hold my right hand, and the promise from the Psalms was that by *His* right hand, He would save me. *How beautiful!* I thought.

At ten minutes to eight the next morning, Len and our daughter, Linda, who had flown down from Washington, arrived at my hospital room just as an orderly appeared to roll me to the operating room.

"A quick prayer," Len said. He had no sooner said, "Amen" than the telephone rang. It was our dear friend, the Reverend Joe Bishop. "I can't believe this split-second timing," I told him. "The orderly is here to take me to surgery."

"Then time for one more prayer," Joe said. His loving benediction was all around us as we left the room.

All through the corridors Len and Linda walked beside the stretcher, right up to the anteroom.

As I was wheeled into the operating room I was given a beautiful three-part promise, one from each Person of the Trinity:

God the Father would hold me in His everlasting arms.
Jesus would take my right hand in His.
From the moment I lost consciousness, the Holy Spirit would be my
    Breath of life.

After that, suddenly I found that fear was nowhere around.

LL Note: The cyst was benign. Catherine had a recovery as swift and uneventful as the North Carolina doctor predicted.

7

My Yoke Is Easy

*F*or many years I have pondered the following words of Jesus, wanting to bear them out in my life, repeatedly falling short:

> Come to Me, all you who labor and are heavy-laden and over burdened, and I will cause you to rest—I will ease and relieve and refresh your souls.
>
> Take My yoke upon you, and learn of Me; for I am gentle (meek) and humble (lowly) in heart, and you will find rest—relief, ease and refreshment and recreation and blessed quiet—for your souls.
>
> For My yoke is wholesome (useful, good)—not harsh, hard, sharp or pressing, but comfortable, gracious and pleasant; and My burden is light and easy to be borne.
>
> Matthew 11:28–30 AMPLIFIED

Then at age sixty-five I was given a whole new perception of these verses through my friend, Roberta Dorr, author of the novel *Bathsheba*. During a visit at our home, she told me of the miracle-healing of her doctor-husband from supposedly incurable Hodgkins disease.

The diagnosis was made while her husband, David, was still in surgical residency. Having a laid-back temperament, David accepted the verdict of a very limited life span and went about his work.

But Roberta has a different nature—always seeking to understand, always questioning, always a fighter. She resisted the idea of losing her beloved husband and seeing their three small children grow up without a father. She and her husband had just filled out the final papers and were ready for an appointment to a hospital in Africa when the diagnosis was made final. Why, she asked over and over, had this happened?

No answer came. Until at last, with total relinquishment she asked God the right question, "How do You want me to pray about my husband?"

One morning shortly afterward, this thought was planted in her mind: "Pray that your husband will be able to *use* for the good of others the medical training he has been given."

As soon as Roberta prayed *this* prayer, the tremendous burden lifted from her heart. She had discovered that the yoke Jesus offered really did bring peace; by praying *His* prayer, sharing with Him His concern for all of suffering humanity, she was able to repose her load on His great strength. One year later the doctors at Johns Hopkins were astonished during a periodic test to discover no trace of disease in David. They were frank to say that they did not understand what had happened. Three years later, they dismissed him entirely, still unable to explain it. The disease never reappeared, but during the four years of "waiting," David completed a surgical residency that was to change his life. Instead of going to Africa, he went to the Gaza Strip where he was desperately needed as a surgeon.

It was while the Dorrs were on a medical mission to the Middle East that Roberta had further illumination about what it means to be yoked together with Jesus. (The Dorrs spent a total of seventeen years in

Yemen and Gaza.) Perhaps seeing double-yoked oxen working the fields helped bring the truth home to her.

Roberta had always thought of these verses in Matthew as a metaphor of Jesus helping her with *her* projects, *her* life—plowing *her* field, so to speak.

Then one day the Lord said to her something like this: "No, you have it all wrong—backwards. Drop your plans. At the beginning of each day simply ask to be yoked with Me for *My* work, to plow *My* field. Then you will find that the yoke fits perfectly and that the burden truly is light."

I've thought a lot about Roberta's experience. First, David's healing. Did it happen in part because David was so involved in ministering to other people that he didn't have time to dwell on his own illness? Did he not only find refreshment in serving his Lord, but healing as well?

Not the whole answer, of course, but a clue toward that great mystery of how and why miraculous healings take place.

Second, there's much for me to ponder about the injunction Roberta received to "drop her plans" and listen for God's plan for her.

Again I'm back to relinquishment. Time after time I've laid my concerns, questions, doubts, plans, on God's altar. The problem for me is leaving them there.

At age sixty-five I still have that determination to take charge of my life, to prove that I can still do everything I did when I was twenty. I still want God to applaud my good works. It's so ridiculous! No wonder I have trouble sleeping and breathing.

Meanwhile, God waits patiently for me to come to Him, forgetting my agenda, so that I can hear what He has in mind for me.

Is it possible for an opinionated woman in her autumn years to become like a child and sit at the feet of Jesus with one idea—to hear what He will say?

8

The Joy of the Lord
Shall Be Your Strength

*F*or weeks now I have been so discouraged about the quality of my writing that I wonder if I am capable of doing another novel. Is *Christy* to be the only one?

The new novel I've been working on is set in western Pennsylvania during the 1930s. So far it seems lifeless. The characters aren't real to me yet.

Yesterday was the low point as I struggled to get words on paper. I had a mental picture of myself as a lost, crying sheep at the bottom of a very deep pit. Then with startling clarity these words of Jesus flooded my thinking:

I tell you the truth, I am the gate for the sheep . . . whoever enters through me will be saved. He will come in and go out, and find pasture.

John 10:7–9 NIV

How like Jesus to rescue people like me, not because we have done, or are currently doing, one solitary thing to deserve it. I sought Him and last night He reached down and, with His shepherd's crook, physically and spiritually lifted me out of the pit. Today He is comforting me even as He puts renewed strength into me.

It happened through a dream, fragments of which remained in my mind upon awakening.

In the dream I had a basket in my hands decorated around the rim and sides with flowers and leaves. I was having to "redo" the decorations. As I took off the old ones I was surprised to find how easy they were to remove. But there was an even greater surprise: I *expected* the flowers to be artificial ones, but found them not only real flowers, but surprisingly fresh.

When I awoke there was a joy and a release springing from deep in my spirit and my heart was full of praise.

The message of the dream appeared to be not only my own readiness to begin work on the novel again, but even divine approval of the timing. And the ease with which the bunches of flowers were removed from the basket and the fact that they were *fresh*, seemed to say, "The task of revision will not be as difficult as you have thought, and you will find the material fresh."

I have long known that my writing is never truly on target unless I feel at some point, while in the process of getting words on paper, that certain hallmark of joy within. The scene I am attempting to write may be quite a serious one, but the touchstone of joy must be there—or else I'm working in my own strength, not His.

It will take a little while to turn around a habit of negative thinking about this book—but Jesus is beginning to do that for me this morning. In fact, He who *always* gives to us "more abundantly than we could ask or think" has given me a glimpse of *His* vision for this novel.

I had been realizing the last few days, as I have been doing a quick rereading of the words already written, that I am at the same point in this book I was with *A Man Called Peter* when I received the devastating critique: "You haven't yet gotten *inside* the man Peter."

It was after I fell into a pit of discouragement over that remark that God told me, "No man's life has ultimate significance apart from what that man's life shows about God." So I re-outlined Peter's story *that* way.

Now God is telling me to think of the novel like this: We are living in a time when evil and trouble seem rampant. Every person I know has *trouble* of some kind.

So I am to separate the strands of the different kinds of trouble in the novel, and see what God's solution is to each one. For instance, we have

> Economic trouble—I am writing of the Depression times, the 30s.
> Emotional depression—Ken, the father, with his conviction that he is a failure.
> Ecological trouble—powerful financial interests ignore environmental danger signs.
> Natural disaster—the final flood. What is God saying here? To us today?

I'm going to have to listen to the Inner Voice *very* carefully to "get" all this, but praise God, oh, how I praise Him for this revelation! For He is saying, "Yes, yes, of *course* I want you to write this book. Yes, yes, it has an important message for our time."

Oh, thank You, Lord. Thank You for the return of joy to my life!

9

The Intercessors

Yesterday this Scriptural passage seemed to leap out at me:

> And he [the Lord] saw that there was no man, and wondered that there was no intercessor. . . .
>
> Isaiah 59:16 KJV

Then came a rather startling bit of guidance from the Lord (I want to check this out with others). He seemed to be asking me to set up an intercession ministry that would consist chiefly of people with the desire and the faith to pray for others, and the time to devote to it—like many of the elderly, or handicapped, or those who earnestly want to be used by God but can't figure out *how* to be useful within the limitations of family demands, geographical location, etc.

To these intercessors would be forwarded the letters and requests we receive from those who need prayer—with names removed, of course—to whom it could mean everything to know that other people are lifting them up. My conscience hurts me when people write for prayer and I can give so little time to each one, for there are so many.

It would mean an incredible job of collation and feedback, a lot of postage, probably a newsletter with real input on the subject of intercessory prayer. Since this is a phase of prayer about which I know least, I'm surprised the Lord would lay this upon me.

LL Note: This was Catherine's first journal notation (June 1, 1980) about intercessory prayer; her guidance grew stronger with the passing weeks. From this single verse in Isaiah has grown the Intercessors prayer movement, launched in the fall of 1980 as a part of the nonprofit organization Breakthrough, Inc. (Lincoln, Virginia 22078). As of April 1, 1986, there were 1500 intercessors enrolled to handle the thousands of prayer requests received each year. The newsletter (put out eight times a year) was being mailed to 12,000 people involved in intercession.

Section Five

Spiritual Warfare

*E*arly in our marriage Catherine and I went through periods when we seemed to be up against a kind of unexplained opposition: there would be a series of breakdowns in our household equipment; times when all the children misbehaved for no apparent reason; work would be constantly interrupted; and we would feel a heaviness in our spirits. At first we tried to examine these happenings logically; then as we learned more about the dark powers and principalities at work in the world we realized that on occasion we were under a form of satanic attack.

When Catherine was writing Beyond Our Selves, she reported the spirit of opposition in her office as being almost palpable. No wonder, since this book more than any other of hers helped people move from unbelief or an uncertain faith into making a commitment to Jesus Christ as Lord.

As we learned more about "the enemy" and his cohorts, we were able to pray against those dark spirits, reducing their effectiveness. But we were never free from them. In fact as the years went by, we accepted the fact that for all of us engaged in Christian service, there is never-ending spiritual warfare.

In the final years of her life, as her body weakened from a series of ailments, Catherine had a daily battle with the dark forces. Rebuking the enemy in the name of Jesus was the best weapon for reclaiming the creative atmosphere to do our work, to minister to others, to protect our home environment.

But we could never relax our vigilance.

LL

I

Fear

*L*ast night I had a vivid dream. . . . While driving a car, I became terrified of what was ahead. With no clear idea of what the problem was, I could not seem to keep from doing the very worst thing possible—*closing my eyes as I drove.*

Then I was driving over a concrete road with about three inches of very clear water on it. There was still overwhelming fear in me. I awoke in panic.

As I pondered it this morning, the message of the dream would appear to be that my actual danger is very small—shallow water. Thus my real problem is fear itself. Fear of many things, including God Himself.

He scolded me for this—gently—this morning, reminding me that fear is one of Satan's tools. The *fear of God*—the wrong kind, that is, fearfulness rather than awe—is something I have struggled with for so many, many years. And I sense that many believing people are like me, unable to love and praise their Heavenly Father fully because of fear—often a fear of punishment.

Then I remembered something that Jesus did. Knowing that all people struggle with fear, He often prefaced what He was about to say to His fellow humans with the words, "Fear not."

Therefore my prayer is, "Lord, I hand my fears over to You, fears of all kinds. Fear of You is actually a kind of blasphemy against Your character. I'm sorry. Forgive me."

In answer to my prayer, a line from an old hymn, "Take it to the Lord in prayer," began running through my mind. The Spirit said very clearly, "Why do you think I am reminding you of these words? *Pay attention to every line of these verses.* Learn to bring everything directly to Me instead of allowing so many worrying wonderings."

What a Friend we have in Jesus
All our sins and griefs to bear!
What a privilege to carry
Everything to God in prayer.
O what peace we often forfeit,
O what needless pain we bear,
All because we do not carry
Everything to God in prayer.

Have we trials and temptations?
Is there trouble anywhere?
We should never be discouraged—
Take it to the Lord in prayer.
Can we find a friend so faithful
Who will all our sorrows share?
Jesus knows our every weakness—
Take it to the Lord in prayer.

Are we weak and heavy-laden
Cumbered with a load of care?

Precious Saviour, still our refuge—
Take it to the Lord in prayer.
Do thy friends despise, forsake thee?
Take it to the Lord in prayer;
In His arms He'll take and shield thee—
Thou wilt find a solace there.

Joseph Scriven (1819–1886)

2 _____

Fear of Death _____

A visit from Betty Malz this week has forced me to do something I keep putting off—examining my attitude about death.

After returning to life from twenty-eight minutes of being dead (*My Glimpse of Eternity*), Betty is so full of *details* of what life will be in eternity, as well as bubbling over with stories of remarkable answers to prayer, that being with her is like a feast.

Yet our conversation several nights ago highlighted my own wrong emotional orientation to death. Though I know intellectually that Jesus *did* conquer death, though I believe with my mind in immortality, my emotions deny this. Somewhere back in my childhood certain experiences planted firmly the conviction that death is our enemy, to be hated and fought every step of the way. By the

time I was in my teens, I was writing poetry full of emotional
rebellion about the brevity of our lives here and how pathetically
unfair that is.

I slept almost none at all night before last, finding in myself a deep
unrest about all this.

Yesterday morning as I prayed about it, I remembered a New
Testament verse about those "who for fear of death are in bondage all
their lives." This seemed such an exact description of me that I thought,
I'd like to take a look at that verse. Whereupon the Helper clearly said (in
my thoughts), *Look in Hebrews.*

So I turned to that book, not having the least idea *where* in Hebrews. I found the verse in the second chapter, fifteenth verse.

Verse fourteen talks about what Jesus did for us on the Cross:

. . . that by [going through] death He might bring to nought and
make of no effect him who had the power of death, that is, the devil.

Verse fifteen:

And also that He might deliver and completely set free all those who
through the (haunting) fear of death were held in bondage throughout the whole course of their lives.

AMPLIFIED

How to the point! I decided that I had been in emotional bondage
to the fear of death long enough, that Satan had used this as a way of
stirring up doubt and confusion in me. All of which has interfered
with my having full fellowship with the Father.

So I made a date with Betty Malz and Len for 4:30 yesterday
afternoon and in prayer together we claimed my freedom, asking that
Jesus fulfill His promise "to deliver and completely set free."

Last night at the church meeting where Betty spoke, one of the
hymns we sang was "Be Still, My Soul." The words were like a Night
Letter straight from the heart of God in answer to my claiming prayer
in the afternoon (italics added).

Be still, my soul—the Lord is on thy
   side!
Bear patiently the cross of grief or pain;
Leave to thy God to order and provide—
In every change He faithful will remain.

Be still, my soul—thy best, thy Heavenly
   Friend
Through thorny ways leads to a joyful
   end.

Be still, my soul—thy God doth undertake
To guide the future as He has the past,
Thy hope, thy confidence let nothing
   shake—
All now mysterious shall be bright at
   last. . . .

3

Self-dissatisfaction

Last night I dreamed I was making a telephone call from a department store pay phone. There was immense trouble, though, about finding the number. I could not locate the yellow pages of the directory. Then I thought that I might have the number written in one of two notebooks in my handbag. But the two notebooks kept getting mixed up, and as I would find the page, someone else would push into the phone booth ahead of me, and my finger would slip out of place in the little notebook. Once I located the number, only to find it so blurry that I could not read it.

The message my unconscious seems to be playing back to me— confusion. Not enough order in my life, or even in my pocketbook.

This morning as I sought answers in prayer to a number of prob-

lems, the same spirit of confusion seemed to settle upon me. Quickly
I asked for His help. After a few moments I was led to Psalm 78.
These verses hit me:

> He divided the sea and led them through. . . . He guided them
> with the cloud by day and with light from the fire all night. He split
> the rocks in the desert and gave them water as abundant as the
> seas. . . . But they continued to sin against him rebelling in the
> desert against the Most High. They willfully put God to the test by
> demanding the food they craved.
>
> vv. 13–18 NIV

> . . . and his wrath rose against Israel, for they did not believe in
> God or trust in his deliverance.
>
> vv. 21–22 NIV

Was I full of doubts and questions and criticism like the Israelites?
Yes, I had to admit I was. How can I be free of this, Lord?

These words of reassurance came:

"Thou art my beloved child, Catherine. Rest in that love. . . .
Simply rest in it. Bathe in it. Stop asking so many questions. Stop all
this probing, taking your spiritual temperature. Does the Lord want
me to do this? Or that? Is this right? Is that right? This is the source
of the confusion you are feeling.

"You *are* My child, My disciple. I accepted you long ago—*as you
are*—as you are growing.

"You are *still* accepted. Nothing is between us from My side, only
yours! Grasp that by faith and all else will follow.

"The nervous probing is Satan's doing, to unsettle you, to confuse
you, to knock you off the base of your belief.

"Let My joy flow through you unimpeded, even though you do not
feel it at first. *Let it flow. Be not afraid.* That joy will sweep away your
fear and uncertainties.

"Stop accusing yourself, Catherine. Turn any such thoughts over to
Me instantly. They come from Satan, not from Me.

"Place yourself in My hands as though you were an infant. Let *Me* handle your questions, the tattered remnants of your unbelief, your growth in My *grace*—not My stringency.

"Grace . . . grace . . . grace. Love . . . love . . . love. I came *not* to judge or to condemn. *All* accusation comes from the enemy.

"Open the floodgates that My love can bathe you and that the living water may flow through you to others."

4

Free from Bondage

Sarah, a woman in our Tuesday night group at church, told us the following experience.

For years she had been struggling to quit smoking. She would get down to two packs a week, then back up to three, endlessly defeated. Her conscience hurt her about the grip that cigarettes had on her.

Sarah sat on the front row the night Len did a Bible study on how the Holy Spirit can free us from any habit that binds us and keeps us from a close relationship to Jesus. The Scripture he focused on:

> For if you live according to the sinful nature, you will die; but if by the Spirit you put to death the misdeeds of the body, you will live,

because those who are led by the Spirit of God are sons of God.

Romans 8:13–14 NIV

In his talk, Len included alcohol, drugs, cigarettes, food, and sex as pitfalls for the compulsive personality. Sarah told us later that she began to associate Len with her cigarette struggle.

One night Sarah had a short, vivid dream in which Len was present. Then she saw a hand with a lighted cigarette between the fingers. The fingers began vigorously and repeatedly tamping out the cigarette. With that the dream ended.

When Sarah awoke the next morning she pondered whether the meaning of the dream could be as obvious as it seemed. Scarcely thinking, she reached for her package of cigarettes. There was a single cigarette left. She lighted it, but it tasted different, not at all good. She tamped it out and has had no desire to smoke since. Her tastes, her desire-world itself, had been transformed by the Spirit.

Later Len and I shared with the group the following steps we use in praying for someone in the grip of addiction:

1. In the name of Jesus move against the powers of darkness that have attached themselves to R———'s mind and will.

2. With Christ's authority, drive these forces back a day at a time. Persist. No matter how long it takes; refuse to be discouraged.

3. Once you have captured any piece of ground in R———'s mind from the enemy, occupy it with a declaration of faith, telling Satan he cannot return.

4. When R——— has been released from an addiction, pray for his salvation and his infilling by the Holy Spirit.

We also suggested that anyone who, like Sarah, has been released from addiction, hold onto the following verse:

Stand fast therefore in the liberty wherewith Christ hath made us free, and be not entangled again with the yoke of bondage.

Galatians 5:1 KJV

5

Satan's Best Weapon ─────────

There is an oft-repeated story about the time Satan gathered his co-workers together for a strategy session. The purpose: find more effective ways to tempt Christians into sin.

One evil spirit said, "Let's set before them the delights of sin."

Satan shook his head. "That works up to a point, but not with the strong believers."

Another incubus suggested, "We can show them that virtue is costly."

Satan again shook his head. "They know that the rewards are worth it."

The third little demon had a knowing look in his eye. "Let's bring discouragement to their souls."

"Now you have it!" cried Satan. "Discouragement is the weapon!"

How true it is! Right now I am worn down by lack of sleep. I thought I had won a victory over sleeplessness and dependence on sleeping pills six years ago. But lately I've been in the pit of despair. Nor has going back to a mild sleeping pill helped.

This morning I want to put on paper what it is like to try and sleep. I go to bed fatigued, yet am not able to let go. The sleep mechanism of the frontal lobe of my brain is apparently all askew. It's as if the stay-alert function is working overtime—night and day. Even at moments when, out of total weariness, I am about to drop off, the brain sends the message, "Wake up!" and I jerk to.

There is a constant tiredness behind my eyes, lids are heavy as if pressing the eyes back into the head.

I cannot find any comfortable position in bed. Make elaborate arrangements with pillows and sheet, but no sooner settled than I am moving again. What to do with the arms to keep them from aching? How to place my neck?

My face itches and I must scratch. There's a cramp in one leg and I flex and unflex my toes. The sheet is scratching my chin. Right arm is hot. Finally, I tumble to the fact that there can be no sleep until I lie perfectly still for a while. Yet it's agony to force myself to do so.

The nights seem endless. How can they be so long?

When I do—toward dawn—drop off, the "sleep start" wakens me abruptly. A muscle in a leg gives a sudden jerk.

I have come to hate the bed, yet am drawn to it, always hopeful. Isn't it man's *natural* state to sleep? Lord, I'm exhausted and discouraged.

So many times discouragement has been the doorway through which the powers of evil have flooded into my situation. For discouragement says, "My problem is bigger than God, who is not adequate to handle my particular need. So herewith I take my eyes off God, bow down before my problem, and give myself to it."

In digging through Scripture on this subject, I have discovered that no matter how difficult the situation, Jesus' attitude was always a calm, "Courage, My son, My daughter. Have no fear. There is nothing here that My Father cannot handle."

It was not that Jesus minimized the problem, but rather that His faith was a magnet for God's power. He knew that *no* problem was any match for the Lord God Almighty.

I confess now that I am discouraged because I have been relying on myself rather than on You, Lord; I have expected something from myself and am deeply disappointed not to find it there. I want to think that I can handle things myself . . . succeed better . . . do more than others.

In *The Practice of the Presence of God*, Brother Lawrence writes that he was never upset when he had failed in some duty. He simply confessed his fault, saying to God, "I shall never do otherwise, if You leave me to myself; it is You who must hinder my failing and mend what is amiss." After this admission, He gave himself no further uneasiness about it.

What the devil wants us to do, of course, is to focus on our failure rather than on Jesus. For when we keep our eyes on Him, we find that no problem—of the 1st century or the 20th—has ever defeated Him.

Jesus never encountered a human situation that discouraged Him. Sickness and disease? Jesus healed a man blind from birth . . . a woman who'd had an issue of blood for twelve years . . . another bent double with arthritis for eighteen years. At not one of these cases did Jesus look with despairing heart.

Did sin get Him down? Never, no matter how heinous. Jesus insisted that He had come into the world not to condemn us, but to save us (John 8:15; 12:47). His attitude was that any time spent in condemnation, in wallowing in old sins and regrets, in recriminations, in kicking ourselves around, is wasted time.

The woman taken in adultery, He forgave and restored—immediately.

Zaccheus had spent a lifetime in greed and grasping. Yet Jesus told him, "*This* day has salvation come to thy house."

Jesus' word in any situation was one of encouragement:

To the paralytic borne by four: "Courage, My son!"

To the ruler of the synagogue whose daughter was dying: "Have no fear, only believe, and she shall get well."

To Martha, grieving over her dead brother: "Said I not unto thee, that if thou wouldst believe, thou shouldst see the glory of God?"

Hear that, Satan? In the name of Jesus, I kick you and discouragement out of my life.

6

The Other Side of the Mountain

Yesterday David Hill from Dallas telephoned and was on for forty-five minutes. David has had an escape from some sort of cult. He is unmarried, thirty-two or thirty-three, and has been a Christian for eight years. *What* a mature Christian he is for an eight-year-old!

He has had quite a bit of experience with spiritual warfare, and one of the helpful facts he gave me is that when we're engaged in these battles energy is sapped from us and we are *very* prone to depression. *Exactly* my state for the last two months!

He also painted a very vivid picture of Genesis 22. As Abraham and Isaac were toiling up Mount Moriah, Satan must have been tempting

Abraham every few minutes. "Surely you did not hear God correctly! Sacrifice your son and heir? Why should you do such an evil thing? Why, Isaac was God's special gift to you in your wife's old age. You're probably just getting senile, etc., etc."

But at *that very moment* that Abraham was struggling with his thoughts, the ram was traveling up the *other* side of the Mount, and God was preparing the way of escape.

David's message was, God always is working on the "ram part"— the escape, God's own way out.

7

Knowing the Enemy _____

*H*ow much better we will withstand Satan's assaults when we're wise to his tactics! Thus, these past few days I've been searching the Bible for insights as to the forces—within and without—arrayed against us.

The Serpent's Strategy:
First of all the serpent's objective was to call God a liar, to contradict His Word, to tell Eve—and us—"His Word is not so." It was because Eve believed the serpent as over against God that the Fall came (Genesis 3:2–4).

The serpent's second strategy was to tell Eve, in effect, "God is out to take away or withhold something good from you."

The third trick was to tempt the woman into letting the forbidden fruit play upon her senses. She put herself in the way of the temptation, walked around it, looked at it, toyed with it (Genesis 3:6).

Three curve balls—and Eve struck out.

The Immediate Results of her sin:

1. Eve wanted fellowship in her disobedience. She felt at once the sense of isolation that sin brings. Inevitably when we do wrong we want to drag other people down with us. So Eve gave the fruit to Adam to eat (v. 6).

2. Innocence was gone. Both the man and the woman knew they were naked.

3. They had no desire for fellowship with God; ran from Him; in fact, hid themselves from Him (Genesis 3:8).

4. They knew fear (v. 10).

5. They knew shame (vv. 7–10).

6. Each blamed his sin on someone else:

Adam—on Eve (v. 12).

Eve—on the serpent (v. 13).

The Far-reaching Results:

1. Woman is reduced to a subordinate position to man.

2. In sorrow and pain and difficulty will the reproduction process take place. Moreover, woman will be something of a slave to her sexual desire for her husband (v. 16).

3. Man shall till the ground, which will be stubborn in producing for him. He will get food by the sweat of his brow (vv. 17–19).

4. Death enters life—"To dust thou shalt return" (v. 19).

5. Adam and Eve begin to wear clothing, symbol of perpetual loss of innocence (v. 21).

6. They are driven from the Garden and the Tree of Life (vv. 23–24).

How seriously did Jesus take demons?

Apparently very seriously indeed. When He sent the first group of disciples on the first mission, His charge to them was:

First: Preaching
Second: Casting out demons (Mark 3:14–15).
The demons always seemed to have recognized:
1. *Who Jesus was* (Mark 1:24, 34; 3:11; 5:7).
2. *That Jesus was against them all the way.*
3. *That they had to obey Him* (Mark 1:25–28, 5:12–13).

Jesus' dealing with demons:
1. He rebuked them (Mark 1:25).
2. He then gave them a direct order (Mark 1:25, 5:8).
3. He charged them not to reveal who He was (Mark 3:12).

The result for the possessed individual:
1. He is often buffeted and thrown about (Mark 1:26).
2. But the demon obeys Jesus and departs (Mark 1:26).

These further insights have come as I pondered Satan's inroads into my own heart and will:
1. When we rejoice over, or look for, or repeat with relish negative news, then we have placed ourselves on the side of evil.
2. It is possible to take this negative stance so often with regard to situations and persons that this becomes a way of life. Negative thinking is really a weapon of Satan. *We* call it "realism"; Christ calls it "not believing the truth."
3. We do not realize how definitely our mind-set—that is, what the mind picks out from all the news to highlight—reveals *whose* side we're really on.
4. Even after we have accepted Jesus and asked Him to come and live within us, Satan will keep trying to persuade us that the flesh is dominant and must be obeyed. Satan will also feed us the lie that "that's human nature" and there's nothing we can do about it.
5. The response to Satan's attacks has to be *faith*. When I became Jesus' woman, a series of marvelous things happened—whether the effects are visible yet or not. Among them, as I accepted the atoning

work of Jesus for me, I was unshackled on the inside from my bondage to the flesh, freed from the ascendancy of flesh over spirit (Romans 8:2). Paul says that when we accept this wonderful liberation by faith, and begin to live it out, we find that the flesh now *has* to obey the spirit, that Satan has been subdued, overcome, deprived of his power (Romans 8:3). Realizing this, we need only allow the Holy Spirit to lead the way, step by step, obedient act by obedient act, like a conquering General victoriously marching ahead (Romans 8:9–16).

8

Offensive Warfare

Yesterday I read a pamphlet by Ralph Mahoney, editor of *World Map Digest*, who makes the following powerful points about spiritual warfare:

1. "On this rock I will build my church, and the gates of hell will not overcome it" (Matthew 16:18 NIV).

Now, gates are stationary. *They* are fixed in place, stay put. Therefore, the "gates of hell" cannot move against us. So Jesus has to mean that His church is to take the offensive against the citadel of Satan.

The picture (according to Mahoney) is of a victorious Church laying siege to hell and breaking down the gates to release its prisoners.

2. "That enemy of yours, the devil, roams around like a lion roaring [in fierce hunger], seeking someone to seize upon and devour"

(1 Peter 5:8 AMPLIFIED). Peter did not write those words to scare us to death, says Mahoney. For the key word ·is *like* the lion. Satan is always an imitator, a fake, a bluff, a counterfeit. He *isn't* a lion. His claws were drawn out at Calvary.

3. The real Lion is Jesus, "the Lion of the tribe of Judah" (Revelation 5:5 AMPLIFIED). We Christians have no strength or ability in ourselves for fighting Satan, or for pulling down gates, or anything else.

But as we allow the Lion of Judah to live in us, we take on the nature of Him who is the real Lion. Our weapons—fickle and weak of themselves—pass through God and become mighty enough to make hell itself tremble with fear.

9

Conversations with God ___

LL Note: As she learned more and more about confronting Satan with his lies and deceit, rebuking him daily, and seeking to hear the voice of the Lord, the answers from Him became clearer and clearer. Here are excerpts from Catherine's 1981 journal:

"Lord, I need Your help in so many areas. How can I better hear Your voice?"

You need to begin listening in the absolute quiet as you did during that summer long ago on Cape Cod. Remember how you lay on the daybed in the living room, pen and notebook in hand, in absolute stillness? I spoke to you then—and will again.

A morning Quiet Time should be that—not simply reading in this book or that. What I, your Lord, have to say to you is more important than the best wisdom of any author.

"Lord, my novel goes so slowly. The words I put on paper seem so wooden. I need Your Help."

I am glad you have asked Me to be your editor. Turn to Me each time you begin writing for specific directions. If you want real creativity, follow My inner directives.

Now, start reading 2 Corinthians and I'll have more to say to you.

"Lord, I wince at 2 Corinthians 2:9: obedience in all things. How do I achieve that? I feel like such a failure in that area."

Child—you always take life too seriously—with too heavy a spirit, too anxious a mien. A true child of Mine has no need to worry so. You act as if you think you have to do everything yourself, as if I, your Burden Bearer, am not with you at all. Do you really think that honors Me?

Do you not see the egotism in all this? Satan has gotten a toehold in this attitude-area in you, and you have failed to recognize it so that you can deal with it. He is the one who wants you burdened down, fatigued, feeling overwhelmed with work.

"Lord, what a gorgeous revelation! Thank You, thank You. . . . But how do I kick the old boy out and let You turn these wrong attitudes around?"

By recognizing Satan's lies. For example, he wants you to think that your everyday life is monotonous and dull. The very opposite is true. Satan's aim is always to turn your eyes to the world. That's not for you. Even during that brief period in Washington when you thought you were making a little progress into Washington social life, it wasn't for you and would have garnered you husks had you achieved it. Forget it! Permanently! Your life is fascinating, with pleasant surprises every day. Praise Me for the richness of the life I have given you.

Each time you feel a negative attitude building up inside yourself, refuse to accept it. Recognize the satanic source of it, reject it, and turn to Me.

"Lord, there are doubts in me this morning. I admit it. Doubts that what I am writing down here is really You speaking and not just my wishful thinking or what I think You would say. How can I be sure?"

Proof in the world of the spirit never comes in the same way as in the material world. Don't try to transfer the techniques of what you call "evidence" from the one realm to the other.

Trust the Holy Spirit to be the link between us, to speak My words, transfer them to you—and He will. Was there not a sureness and a joy and a knowledge of My benediction on you yesterday that you have not known in a long time?

"Yes, there was, Lord. But there are so many things I want and need to talk over with You that it's going to take all eternity to do it."

Your endless curiosity, which at its best is real seeking, is from Me. Don't fight it. Those who seek Me, do find. Remember? "The poor in spirit". . . . Always I am ready to receive any questing. I bless you and love you beyond comprehension.

"Lord, I know that discouragement is from Satan, that I have no business being discouraged under any circumstances. But I am troubled about my novel. I don't feel I can finish it. How do I keep from giving into those down feelings?"

Patience, Catherine, patience. Don't be dismayed. What's happening to you is only a ripple, a little wave on a big sea. This too will pass. The hostages do come home. The prodigal does return. Joy cometh in the morning.

Take a deep breath, look to Me, and be glad. Smile again. The sky has not fallen in.

In other words, keep at it.

"Thank You, Lord. And thank You that the Spirit gave me this verse from Psalm 31 yesterday: 'My times are in Your hand' (v. 15 AMPLIFIED)."

"Lord, what I read in Tournier's *The Healing of Persons* is exciting to me because I have long sought the answer to the problem of 'scruples,' of why I am the sort of person who is always finding some one little thing wrong in my life that I am convinced stands between me and You. I feel very guilty about having to go back to sleeping pills, even though they are the mildest available. So, Lord, the question I ask today: Am I exaggerating a minor problem, my scruple of the moment—sleeping pills—in order not to have to face up to something much more important that You really want me to look at?"

Do you not see that your love of sleep and your desire to escape into sleep is, in large part—and always has been—because you are reluctant to give more of yourself in love for others?

"What a revelation, Lord! But how do I go about letting You change something as ingrained in me as this? It would be asking You to change a lifelong habit pattern. Also, I'd be afraid that going the people route really would knock out my writing."

I told you that My yoke is easy and My burden is light, didn't I? My burden was and is and always has been love of people, love of you, Catherine. You've never believed Me that this burden is light. You'll find that this is so only as you allow Me to take you by the hand and lead you out. Are you willing?

"Yes, Lord."

"Lord, are there other sins You want me to look at, which I have perhaps avoided facing up to, by the smoke screen of small 'scruples'? What I long for is that love of You, and the realization of Your love for me, become the motivating factor in my obedience."

Ah, if only you knew how much I love you! If only you knew what love surrounds you from the "cloud of witnesses" here with Me—your father, your brother, and Peter. If only you knew how many prayers are constantly flowing for you. How grateful you should be for the waves of good will flowing to you constantly from those who read your books.

Relax into My love. Allow Me to love you. There are times when a mother wants to hold her child. No words need pass between them, just the feel of love. This morning let Me love you like that. Let all spiritual strain and tension go. Relax in Me.

"How beautiful, Lord. I do!"

"Lord, is there any particular word You want to speak to me this morning?"

Your life has become unbalanced, Catherine, hence your boredom. You need to cook, to garden, to shop, to exercise more, to be with people more. The more you retreat into the idea-world away from people, the more unreal your Christianity and your relationship with Me will become—even though in such retreat you might think that you were being more spiritual.

"I had almost no sleep last night, Lord. This morning I am full of fears again."

Read the 91st Psalm, Catherine, and absorb it into your bone and marrow and bloodstream and mind and heart and spirit.

I will deliver Catherine. . . .

I will set her on high because she knows and understands My name, has a personal knowledge of My mercy, My love, My kindness. You, Catherine, are to trust and rely on Me, knowing that I will never forsake you.

You, Catherine, will call upon Me, and I will answer you; I will be with you in trouble, I will deliver you and honor you.

One fearful of the water can never get over the fear by standing on the bank shivering, consumed by the fear. . . .

I will not force one to do anything. . . .

Take the first step toward Me. Trust My love for you. Trust . . . trust!

Section Six

The Final Victory

Early in 1982 Catherine realized her time on earth was limited. The emphysema in her lungs had been slowly reducing her vitality. Walking up a flight of stairs was a major undertaking. Talking to people, meetings, shopping drained her.

Saddest of all to see was how her growing breathlessness affected her mornings, the cream time for manuscript work she looked forward to so much. I would watch her go resolutely into her office at 9:00 A.M. Forty minutes later I would hear her return to our bedroom. Once I confronted her there as she lay listlessly on the bed.

Tears welled up in her eyes. "I try to concentrate," she said. "The inner drive is gone. I don't have it anymore."

Then she would rail at herself for being a quitter, get up, and try again. My dilemma was: Should I prod her into doing what was painful and hard, or let her drift into invalidism?

The answer soon became clear. Catherine's basic competitiveness, her battling nature, her spirit of adventure, and her curiosity about life could not, should not, be allowed to die. Catherine would never have forgiven me if I had encouraged her to let go of all this.

So we waged spiritual war against the forces of darkness and the enemy's subtle enticements to give in to weakness. The coffee-pot alarm continued to be set for 6:30 A.M. The day began with an hour of Scripture reading, prayer, and journal entries. During the morning, work continued on the novel Julie. *Commitments to our prayer and fellowship groups were kept. We ended the day in prayer, when I anointed Catherine with oil, taking a stand against ill health, asking for sharpness of thinking and a healing of body and spirit.*

LL

I

His Unfinished Work in Me

*D*reamed last night about death. I don't relish putting this one on paper, but since it *has* to be worked through with the Lord, I suppose I must.

I was in a country where certain citizens were being exterminated by order of the state. One got one's notice and came to a special "office" in which were three booths, side by side. In one of these you were given a shot, like a dog being "put to sleep." Afterwards you were carted off to a back room where the bodies were stacked.

Apparently my number had come up. When I got to the office, I noticed that there were stacks and stacks of dirty dishes in the three booths. I sought to stall my death by offering eagerly to wash all the dishes. The attendant said, "Sure, go ahead. I don't blame you. Just don't tell any of the others that I agreed."

I started to wash a stack of plates, saying to myself, "There's always the chance of something happening to intervene, a national emergency or something." Then I woke up.

So now that I have put this dream on paper, Lord, what does it mean—and what do I do about it?

As I waited for some response, a name came to mind—*John Wesley.*Tuttle's book on Wesley was in the stack of unread books on my night table. I picked it up and soon discovered that Wesley and I shared a dread of death as the Great Enemy. Wesley's fear surfaced dramatically in 1735 during a crossing of the Atlantic to Georgia. There were heavy storms at sea and the small wooden ship at times seemed doomed. Most on board, including the crew, were terror-struck. The only ones who remained calm were a group of German Moravian Christians.

Seeing the strength of these Christians as they faced death, Wesley knew he must work through his problem. In reviewing his walk of faith, he realized he had espoused a life of *asceticism,* which took four forms:

1. Self-denial. (He lived frugally in order to give money to the poor.)
2. Solitude.
3. Works of charity. (Including visits to the terrible prisons of the time where he prayed with condemned men.)
4. Interior life as exemplified by the great mystics.

Now Wesley had to admit that while each of these disciplines had a place in Christian life, not one of them dealt with his fear of death. Finally he began to see that this fear was not from God, as the mystics maintained, but from Satan.

Soon after these discoveries John Wesley had his personal experience of the Holy Spirit at Aldersgate. He was back against the basic New

Testament proposition: There is no road to God except via faith in the finished work of Jesus Christ on the Cross. Joy flooded in and gradually his fear of death dropped away as the totality of these triumphant words of Jesus sank into his being:

> In My Father's house there are many dwelling places (homes). If it were not so, I would have told you, for I am going away to prepare a place for you.
>
> And when (if) I go and make ready a place for you, I will come back again and will take you to Myself, that where I am you may be also.
>
> John 14:2–3 AMPLIFIED

I know that the Holy Spirit has much unfinished work to do inside me about my attitude toward death. I need this, and I will myself to desire it.

2

Our Servant Role

I was the recipient of a beautiful and touching act last night that reverberates through my prayer time this morning. Myra Gertz, a friend and member of our church fellowship group, asked if she could drop in for a short visit.

As we talked I could see that she had something on her mind and was struggling how to say it. Finally she did.

"Catherine, I feel a bit foolish, but the Lord told me to come over and wash your feet. I don't know what this is all about and I've never done this before, but the Voice was very emphatic."

I was startled. My inner reaction was, *Oh, no! Surely, this is not necessary.* But our group had been learning to respect these nudges from the Spirit. "We certainly want to obey the Lord, Myra," I agreed.

Soon she was on the floor in front of me with towels and a basin of water. She removed my stockings and shoes and gently began washing my feet.

Tears filled my eyes as I felt the presence of the Lord through Myra. He had instigated this, just as He had done with His disciples two thousand years ago.

I was the needy one all right. My fatigue level had never been lower.

"Catherine, the Lord wants you to know He loves you deeply," Myra said as she finished drying my feet. "May I pray for you now?"

"Of course."

She did, asking for a healing in every part of me—mind, spirit, emotions, and body. A deep feeling of peace spread over me. "Thank you for being faithful, Myra," I said as she left.

This morning I read through the Scripture account of this act by Jesus in the New Testament book of John:

> When he has finished washing their feet, (Jesus) put on his clothes and returned to his place. "Do you understand what I have done for you?" he asked them.
>
> "You call me 'Teacher' and 'Lord,' and rightly so, for that is what I am. Now that I, your Lord and Teacher, have washed your feet, you also should wash one another's feet. I have set you an example that you should do as I have done for you. I tell you the truth, no servant is greater than his master, nor is a messenger greater than the one who sent him. Now that you know these things, you will be blessed if you do them."
>
> John 13:12–17 NIV

I have set you an example that you should do as I have done for you. . . . Myra had been obedient to this instruction of Jesus, although I can imagine what she went through, wondering if it would seem over-emotional to me.

And it did, at first. But how I needed it. I was hurting. Jesus knew this, wanted to demonstrate His love for me and chose Myra as His vessel. If she had not been faithful, a beautiful inner healing experience would not have happened.

3

Body Language

I beseech you therefore, brethren . . . that ye present your bodies a living sacrifice, holy, acceptable unto God, which is your reasonable service.

Romans 12:1 KJV

Reading the Bible yesterday afternoon, I felt an inner nudge to stop and reread this verse. I was conscious that I resisted this idea of offering my body as a sacrifice. Why? Because I suspected it could mean more speaking and traveling, more stress and pressure, with consequent loss of sleep at night, and no chance to recoup with daytime naps.

What is so bad about this is that I'm not really trusting the Lord with my physical body—and that's an awful confession. God expects his followers to be willing to be expendable; I've been circling around this point of total trust in a kind of spiritual holding pattern, unwilling to lay down my body as "a living sacrifice." I'm constantly protecting myself, succumbing too quickly to the temptation to stop my work and lie down for a while.

The conviction then came that I must be willing—and tell God so—to have the self with which I was born, the particular bundle of talents, predispositions, preferences, tastes—all that constitutes me—nailed to the Cross with Jesus, actually die and be buried with Him.

But, a voice inside me argued, *didn't I do just this when I became a Christian?* Jesus assured me, however, that this was a new step of dying to the self that so loves body comforts and beautiful things, that longs to escape the demands and entanglements of other people.

Much of that self *I dislike* (Romans 7:15–25). But a lot of what constitutes "me" I like very much. I've been "me," and lived with "me," and put up with "me" a long time. To lay this self on the altar would indeed be a death.

I remembered Jesus' words about "counting the cost" (Luke 14:28). Was I really willing to take myself to the Cross, die and be buried—not having any idea what sort of person would rise with Jesus on the third day?

I went through agony thinking about this, with a lot of tears.

Scripture says that Jesus resolutely and willingly turned His face to the Cross for "the joy that was set before Him" (Hebrews 12:2).

I finally told Jesus that I was going forward with this because I knew He *was* going to have His way with me, now or in the next life.

I got down on my knees in my office by the daybed at 4:40 P.M. and offered up my body to Him as a living sacrifice.

As a result, I must now be obedient hour by hour, day by day, and *not* hold back. This means seeing the indwelling Spirit so residing in my mortal flesh that I am willing to spend myself totally for others, as He did. It means letting *all* self go—everything in my desire world—whenever it cuts across His higher priorities.

No wonder we can do no mighty works until the surrender is this complete. Until Jesus has been allowed to come and make His home in me like *that,* I will be praying for others, doing His work, in *my* name and in *my* nature rather than in His.

The apostle John puts it this way:

He laid down His [own] life for us; and we ought to lay [our] lives down for [those who are our] brothers in [Him].

1 John 3:16 AMPLIFIED

LL Note: Six months of creativity followed during which Catherine made an important breakthrough with her novel Julie, *ministered to several in our prayer group, made several speeches. The two of us drove together from Florida to our farm in Virginia for a month, then flew back to Florida to continue work on her novel.*

4

Self-pity

*T*his morning I took to the Lord a matter that has troubled me for the past two years or so. Sudden tears. I've never been a person who cries often. I generally keep my emotions in check, perhaps more than I should. Recently though, bouts of unpredictable weeping.

The Lord has graciously shown me this morning the why of tears being just under the surface of these past weeks—*self-pity*. In reality, I am weeping for myself.

I weep because of what is happening to me physically. First, my energy level has again dropped to such a degree that it is literally a chore to put one foot before the other. Added to that, worse breathlessness than I've ever known. Sometimes even sitting or lying in bed,

I wonder if I'm going to be able to take the next breath. This makes the stairs and hills at Evergreen Farm an agony.

Most puzzling, after years of battling sleeplessness, suddenly I can hardly stay awake. I must check out with the doctor whether this is an overreaction to the new arthritis drug they are giving me.

Or is it possible that, through lack of oxygen to the brain, I am coming into early senility? Hideous thought! For the first time since early girlhood I have no desire to read at night. During church yesterday, I could scarcely keep my eyes open.

Lord, help!

I am led to this verse:

> . . . I know . . . Whom I have believed . . . and I am [positively] persuaded that He is able to guard and keep that which has been entrusted to me and which I have committed [to Him] until that day.
>
> 2 Timothy 1:12 AMPLIFIED

Since self-pity is a sin, then clearly it has to be dealt with as a sin. A sin because since I belong to Jesus, it is He who has control over my life. Thus He overrules everything that He "allows" to happen to me—overrules it for *good*.

My part is to trust Him as a loving Heavenly Father in each of these adverse circumstances. I am to watch expectantly for the "good" . . . the new adventure He has for me . . . the open door I am to go through toward the better way to which He is leading me.

So, given all that, what is there to have self-pity about?

I see that there is a self-discipline to practice during the days ahead: Each time I am tempted toward despairing self-pity, I am to rebuke it, reject it, and turn immediately to praise.

5

Crisis Time _____

*O*n July 9, 1982, Catherine was so weak that we had her taken by
ambulance to Bethesda Memorial Hospital in Boynton Beach, Florida. Tests showed an alarming carbon dioxide content in her body
because of shallow breathing, and she was placed in the Intensive Care
Unit. Respirator tubes led through her mouth to her lungs; she was fed
through an IV tube in her nose. Machines handled all her body
functions. Family members could visit her for no more than fifteen-
minute periods three times a day.

Because the tubes in her mouth and nose made it hard to wear
glasses, she found it difficult to read the small print of her Bible. A
gray 10 by 7-inch notebook that she had filled over the years with
Bible promises (see p. 242) in large handwriting became her spiritual
lifeline.

The prognosis for her recovery was not good. Doctors could offer no hope that her breathing capacity would improve enough for her to be taken off the respirator. It appeared that Catherine's last days would be spent in the Intensive Care Unit, unable to speak, communicating only through a note pad. Here is a sample of her scribbled comments as the painful weeks passed:

I never knew how frustrating it can be not to be able to speak a word.

I can only move my head about six inches because of that tube in my nose. Lying all night in that one position is torture.

Each little thing is so difficult. It's tough to be getting weaker and weaker and thinner and thinner.

The progress from day to day depends on the blood gases test they take . . . they're running out of places on my arms to draw blood, I bruise so easily.

Remember those old-fashioned cardboard fans people used in church? See if you can find one at home. It gets so hot here at night.

This has been a lonely day. Shifting personnel each with little knowledge of my situation. Sense some are hostile toward Christians. Wish I was a better witness to them for Jesus.

I'm taking twice as many breaths per minute as I should. How do I retrain my body?

I feel that something has to give today. I'm so miserable that I don't see how I can take much more.

It seemed that the Lord was promising me last night that Romans 8:28 would be fulfilled and that I was to begin praising Him. "I believe. Help my unbelief."

Had a crisis with the IV. They spent two hours trying to get it to work. When I began praying they found the answer.

Prayed about my dread of nights. Discovered why I can't really relax. I'm a chronic thinker and a "what-if-er." Prayed to change.

Imagine, four weeks without a shampoo! I dare not look in the mirror. Will be horrified.

Last night the simple thought, "Be still and know that I am God," pulled me through.

On July 24 at 7:30 A.M., my telephone rang: a male nurse reported that Catherine wanted to see me right away. "Don't be alarmed," he said. "It's not a medical emergency. Your wife has something to tell you that she feels is important."

I awoke Peter and Jeff (the family members then on hand) and we drove immediately to the hospital. Catherine greeted us with great excitement in her eyes and reported through written notes that during the night she had felt the Lord's presence there in her Intensive Care cubicle! With His presence came the assurance that she was being healed.

Confirmation came in the next blood tests, which showed a definite decrease in the carbon dioxide content in her body. Day by day the improvement continued. Just as doctors had been unable to explain Catherine's sudden loss of breathing capacity, so too were they baffled when it returned. One doctor said it had to be the power of prayer.

One by one the tubes came out. The ventilator was wheeled away. On August 11, Catherine was moved out of the Intensive Care Unit; she had been there thirty-two days. Nine days later, on August 20th, a rejoicing husband brought her home.

Catherine had been through a dehumanizing process in Intensive Care and had lost twenty-five pounds. The recuperation was agonizingly slow as members of the family took turns coming to Florida to help her recover. Meanwhile, Catherine resumed her journal entries.

LL

6

Crucified with Jesus

*I*n many ways my thirty-two-day stint in the Intensive Care Unit of Bethesda Hospital was a crucifixion experience. Soon after I arrived there, the Lord reminded me of the act I had performed (through Romans 12:1) of offering forever my defective body, along with all my faculties, as a living sacrifice on His Cross.

While lying on my back, hour after hour, unable to read or talk, I had plenty of time to reflect on the study I did awhile ago on the "Humanity of Jesus." Through it I saw that His humanness for thirty-three years on earth was *real;* that He was as helpless, as "out of control" of circumstances, as we are. All this was in order for Him to be the Wayshower, the true and very practical Captain of our salvation.

I also perceived that during this earthly walk, *the* guiding principle of Jesus' life was "what pleases My Father in heaven, never what *I* want to do."

In the intervening months since I made this study, several things have been happening: (1) the Holy Spirit has been doing a steady softening and melting process within me. This has meant that the plights of other persons presented to me, mostly through correspondence, have been laid on my heart with a new urgency; (2) During this same period my own circumstances have not only been taken out of my control, but also have gone in directions contrary to anything *I* would wish.

At what point in the Christian walk are we *actually* "crucified with Him?" At what point is the mortal self dead on His cross and buried with Him?

In my case, I concluded, dying to self has been going on for some time. For me it has been a slow, torturous, lingering death indeed— no doubt because I have been resisting all the way. I'm reasonably sure that it need not be this drawn out and this painful, if the believer really understands what is going on and why, and assents to it in his will. Yet I do think it's something we have to walk through all the way and *feel*. Death on a Cross hurts.

Early the morning of July 24 (fifteen days after entering the hospital) the climax came for me. I was in a semiconscious, dreaming state when I felt myself literally hanging on the Cross with Jesus. There was no pain from the nails in my hands or feet; only a suffocating, crushing weight on my chest as my entire body dragged downwards. I knew I was close to death, but strangely there was absolutely no fear.

As the weight on the rib cage grew unendurable, however, I was aware of a dark presence, as well as that of Jesus. A fierce struggle with some evil force ensued. Again and again I rebuked the dark power and ordered him to be gone. He didn't leave easily, but leave he did at last.

Then—so gently—Jesus picked me up and removed me from the Cross. As He did so, three words came to me: "The Great Exchange." Later I realized this is what theologians call "the substitutionary atonement," meaning that every sinful thing in our lives was dealt with in Christ's finished work on His Cross. At the moment I knew only that the crushing weight had lifted from my ribs.

I awoke the next morning very excited, feeling that a miracle had taken place in my body. This is the note saved by Len I wrote to the nurse:

> Please grant me this one request! I want to see my family, now! My husband first. Please call him. 732-6352.
>
> My husband, my son Peter, my son Jeffrey. I want all of them. I want no medication before they get here. I'll 'calm down' to suit you.

When Len, Peter, and Jeffrey arrived, through notes I told them about my death, that at one point in my struggle with that dark force, it seemed my body parts were burnt up and lying in pieces around the room. The turning point came when way down deep I cried, "Jesus! Lord. My Lord." And He came and was with me. And He healed me.

My family was very responsive, but I think they wondered if it was an hallucination brought on by low oxygen levels in the brain. The key would be the next blood gases test.

When the doctor arrived at my bedside the next day, he was all smiles. "The carbon dioxide is way down!" he reported. And then we all celebrated!

What transpired on the Cross two thousand years ago has taken on sparkling new meaning for me. We are accustomed to thinking that Jesus carried only our sins on the Cross, but Scripture makes it equally clear that He bore all our sicknesses and diseases there too. . . .

> When evening came, they brought to Him (Jesus) many who were under the power of demons, and He drove out the spirits with a word, and restored to health all who were sick; And thus He fulfilled what was spoken by the prophet Isaiah, He Himself took our weaknesses and infirmities and bore away our diseases.
>
> Matthew 8:16–17 (Isaiah 53:4) AMPLIFIED

Len asked me the other night what I considered the chief significance of my crucifixion experience.

"I'm not sure yet," I replied. "I was close to death and the Lord returned me to life. He must have had a reason."

"Do you know what that might be?"

"There are a number of things I'm supposed to do. Finish my novel was one. Even more important: work on some bruised relationships." Then it struck me. "I've had a crucifixion, but not a resurrection."

Len wouldn't accept this. "You emerged from a dark valley into the light. Wasn't that a resurrection?"

"Not entirely. My breathing was restored to what it was last spring, but that's far from normal. My lungs have still not been completely healed."

"Consider this, Catherine," Len replied. "You've operated with little more than half your normal lung power for almost forty years. But look at all you've accomplished. Maybe, like Paul, God's given you a thorn in the flesh for a reason."

Lord, how much more I have to learn!

7

Doing Grief Work

*H*ow grateful I am for Robert Bonham's[1] visits during my recuperation! What a sensitive counselor and friend! His gifts of wisdom and discernment are balm to my spirit.

After I told him how discouraged I am over the slowness of my recovery and the suspicion that my voice may be permanently damaged, it came out last week that Bob feels I am doing *grief* work.

The minute he spoke the word "grief," it rang a bell within me. He said that whenever we encounter a major shift or change in life,

---

[1] At the time the Reverend Robert Bonham was Director of the Christian Institute of Healing at New Covenant Church, Pompano Beach, Florida.

of necessity it involves separation from things well-known and comfortable (whether completely desirable or not), and this entails
loss.

When I asked him to spell this out as he saw it in my situation, he
ticked off the following:

> *Loss of identity in the Intensive Care Unit (ICU)*. Rings, bracelets, etc.,
> removed and placed in hospital safe. Only individuation is a plastic
> identification bracelet on patient's left wrist.

> *Loss of dignity*. Emergency conditions in ICU rule out privacy. Ten-
> dency on part of nurses is to deal with bodies not persons.

> *Loss of speech for so long*. Respirator tubes in mouth mean communi-
> cation is curtailed.

> *The possibility of loss of life*. Death is common and frequent in ICU.
> Dependency on machines underscores the fragility of life.

> *Loss of mental ability and memory*. Reduced oxygen in brain brings on
> confusion.

As he talked a flood of emotion ran through me. I saw the physical
stripping of possessions that takes place in any hospital as more devastating than I had acknowledged. It says, in part, that any so-called
success one has had is now of no consequence. That comes off too.
Raiment is a hospital gown—the same garment for everyone. One is
just a *body* headed for life or death.

I know now what my husband Peter meant when he was asked what
he had learned from his first heart attack. His reply, "I have learned
that the kingdom of God can go on without Peter Marshall."

In the same way I learned in the hospital that everyone can get along
quite well without my opinions or "insights" or teaching. Even my
wedding ring, symbol of marriage to Len, the closest earthly relationship, was taken away. The experience left me feeling not only helpless
but worthless—a digit. The danger here, of course, is that this sense
of nonentity can lead one into the pit of despair. It can render one

unable not only to accept God's unqualified love, but also the love of other people.

Bob's complete assurance that "this too will pass" was very heartening. He had no answer, though, to my question as to what I can do to make the grief work shorter. Simply that I am to trust God and listen.

This morning I had this word from the Spirit. He tells me to praise and rejoice. He brings to mind the Scripture song we've sung so often at church:

> Rejoice in the Lord always; again I will say Rejoice.
>
> Philippians 4:4 RSV

Rejoice!

That I can enjoy music again through my stereo record-player. I actually got up and played the piano a bit—"Breathe on me, breath of God. . . ."

Rejoice!

Telephoned T. and confessed my lack of love and understanding about several matters. A time of renewed fellowship and reconciliation.

Rejoice!

For patient Len and faithful family . . . for the Intercessors . . . for all who prayed . . . for my doctors and the hospital personnel.

Rejoice!

Linda and I are so close now. She drove down to be with me for a week, bringing a gift of four mats and four napkins for the dining-room table. "Use them," she urged. The point is that Len and the doctor have insisted on my getting out of bed and eating at the table.

Rejoice!

Mary Moncur discovered a tree with mangos out of season. Also fresh grapefruit. And our lime tree is so full that Mary will spend all morning squeezing and freezing them.

Praise You, Lord, for Bob Bonham giving up half of every Saturday to be with me.

Praise You, Lord, for bringing out all the fears that are clinging around the fear of death—so that I can deal with them.

Praise You, Lord, for allowing me to have those experiences in Intensive Care, and for pulling me back from death.

8

Receiving Love

*G*od continues to heal me. This morning He gave me a walloping message about the fact that I have not always been able to receive other people's love and so cannot receive Jesus' love. This revelation was sparked by a hassle with Len last night in our bedroom when I was complaining about members of the household who are shielding me about family situations, finances, and decisions that involve my manuscripts and affairs.

Len became quite agitated; finally with tears in his eyes he said, "Catherine, the doctors have told us that you need time to recover from being at death's door. What we're doing is for your protection, out of our love for you. Don't you realize that we almost lost you?"

With that, his voice broke with a show of emotion such as I have rarely seen in our marriage.

This morning I awoke with the full impact of Len's deep feeling sweeping over me. How often, I wondered, do men in our society shortchange themselves and their families by letting a "macho" front cover up a sensitive nature underneath? The conviction came too, though, that I have not been open enough to love. I've often had trouble accepting the feelings Len did express. The affection and gratitude of friends and readers, too.

"Read 1 Corinthians 13," the Spirit nudged.

Those verses lay it out for me even more stringently than Len did last night:

> Love is patient, love is kind. It does not envy, it does not boast, it is not proud. It is not rude, it is not self-seeking, it is not easily angered, it keeps no record of wrongs. Love does not delight in evil but rejoices with the truth. It always protects, always trusts, always hopes, always perseveres.
>
> 1 Corinthians 13:4–7 NIV

I see further that, while my act of laying my body on the altar as "a living sacrifice" was a good first step, it was not enough for: "Though I give my body to be burned and have not love, it profiteth me nothing" (v. 3).

Now comes further revelation, even as I write. Following the 1944 experience of Jesus' healing Presence in my room after I was bedridden for almost three years, I nevertheless lacked something. I've always supposed it was sufficient faith to make the healing complete.

But suppose it was *love* that was missing, not faith. Oh, obedience was not altogether there either, but obedience would have followed love.

"Lord, I rejoice. Lord, I capitulate. Lord, let Your love—and Len's and the love of those around me, each member of my family, and all the love of far-flung friends through my books—*take over.*"

9

Grief Work Continued—
The Healing of Memories

*T*oday I shared with Bob Bonham what I have only flicked at with Len: that is the strange negativism I'm feeling about myself. Lately I keep seeing the underside of things, tend to concentrate on the downbeat.

I'm aware too of a loosening of the hold that *things* have on me. I could care less about fixing up Evergreen Farm or the Florida house—redecorating, repairing, restoring—whereas I used to be very much on top of all of this.

Bob interpreted these observations positively by telling me that this is a normal part of recuperation, that the "grief work" needs to go on.

He sees too that God is showing me how to *die to self*. The indifference to *things* is simply one manifestation of this. As the culmination of this process, Bob sees that self will eventually be given back to me in a new way.

Even as I write this, the Spirit gives me a further insight—I am to take the lassitude, the wanting to lie down and take oxygen, the lack of motivation and will power to get on with diaphragm exercises, as part and yet another proof of this "death." The crucifixion experience at the hospital was real.

The above, positively seen, is that Catherine is dead and my dependence upon *Jesus'* motivation and *His* strength is more real than ever.

After reassuring me that my negativism is a part of the recovery process, Bob Bonham then sought to lead me through the healing of some memories that lie at the root of my fear of physical death.

Bob asked me to begin this session by seeking "contact" with Jesus. For example, I might ask to feel the touch of His hand on mine. Then I was to let Jesus lead me back to the memory He wanted to heal.

The first one, curiously, was the time I was walking in the woods as a young girl and stepped on something in the leaves. To my horror I saw that it was a dead bird. The dread of that experience has obviously clung to me ever since.

The second was the time our family went to a relative's funeral in Johnson City, Tennessee. The body of Uncle John Herndon was in a coffin open for viewing. This was my first look at a dead person. The stark coldness of my uncle's face numbed me.

The third was a real surprise—the "living death" of my grandmother Sarah Wood for whom I was named. Grandmother, for the last part of her life, stayed in her bedroom, where she would allow no window opened. To me she appeared sealed in a tomb.

Bob had me continue to seek contact with Jesus who repeatedly reassured me that death was a doorway experience, that the body was shed as an old, worn-out garment while the inner person, the essential being, went joyously through the door into eternal life.

The whole process took over an hour.

After Bob Bonham left I remembered that Agnes Sanford in her book *The Healing Gifts of the Spirit* had a chapter entitled "The Healing of the Memories." I found the book in my library, turned to that chapter and was stopped by this sentence:

"The truth is that any wound to the soul so deep that it is not healed by our own self-searching and prayers is inevitably connected with a subconscious awareness of sin."

We find the same connection in the Bible! Jesus died for our *sins*. Yet in Isaiah 53:4 we are told, "Surely he hath borne our griefs."

So there is a sense in which sin equals, or is tantamount to, grief.

Which is why the healing of memories is bound up with the forgiveness of sins.

While pondering all this, I recalled my mother's statement to me several years ago, how it distressed her, after Peter's death, the way I would spend hours talking over lofty "spiritual matters" with our housekeeper while my nine-year-old son, Peter John, playing alone in his bedroom, desperately needed my attention, time, and love.

A picture came to mind. It is an actual photo. Peter John is half-squatting on the floor of his bedroom, his toys around him, his big eyes solemn, bewildered, seeking.

With sudden tears I confessed my "heavenly-mindedness" as a sin and asked Jesus' forgiveness.

Next I asked Jesus to go back in time and take that little boy with the hurt, bewildered eyes in His arms. Then to sit there on the bedroom floor beside him, playing with him, ministering the healing needed to Peter John's lonely heart.

"Thank You, Lord, that all time—past, present, and future—is 'right now' with You. Therefore, that little boy is available to Your healing presence, even as the little girl Catherine is. I claim especially Your power to 'cleanse me from all unrighteousness.' Thank You for Your great promise 'to restore . . . the years that the locust has eaten' (Joel 2:25 AMPLIFIED), both for Peter and for me."

After this prayer I felt the love of Jesus washing over my body like a benediction.

What the Spirit has been doing for me through Bob Bonham is

remarkable. Each time I believe I have plumbed the depths of peace and joy in the Christian life, there is more . . . more . . . more! My spirit bounds and leaps and overflows with thanksgiving so that I struggle for any way at all to express it! The fact that Jesus would love each individual *that much*—me—regardless of worth, regardless of performance turned in, regardless of anything, is *so* amazing. No wonder He was raised to the right hand of the Father and crowned with glory and honor!!

10

Keeping My Eyes
Upon Jesus

*F*ell on my face yesterday. Breathing was laborious. Did very little walking. Could not do the exercises. Was discouraged and disheartened and bored.

I knew the cause of all this. A letter came from my doctor, putting names and tags to my "chronic" illness for use in Medicare forms. It sounded so final that I began looking at *this,* accepting it, settling down to it.

I also opened the door to fear. Not so much fear of death because I've actually, finally worked through that. This time it was a fear that I would let down the readers of my books who expect me to be an example of victorious faith.

In my session with Bob Bonham we traced the roots of this fear of letting people down, back to my childhood. What came out was that my father's praising me so highly when I played the piano for his prayer meetings, or made top grades in school, eventually created in me the feeling that I *had* to achieve in order to have his love.

As the years passed this feeling was extended to other members of my family, to friends, even to God. Added to this was the belief that because I have been so public in my life as a Christian, if I did not measure up to what Jesus expected of me, I would not only let Him down, but that people "out there" would think less of *Him;* that Jesus' reputation would actually suffer.

Put in so many words, this is obviously ridiculous! But that's what came out. So yesterday was a total setback for me.

This morning I sought the Lord's forgiveness and was told something like this, most emphatically:

"Catherine, take your eyes off yourself, off your symptoms, off your fears and center your attention on Me. Look at *Me.* Keep looking at Me.

"Allow Me to be your Doctor. This is My will. I *do* know how to give you health. I made you. I know how to mend you.

"Why do you think I healed everyone who came to Me in the days of My flesh? Out of overflowing mercy. I had only to see any human being blind or crippled or sick or in pain to want to set the wrong situation right as quickly as possible.

"I have told you in My Word (Hebrews) that as man's High Priest I am able—and want—to 'run' to the assistance of those who cry to Me."

In my answering prayer, I said, "Lord, I do cry to You. I give You permission to change me on the inside, to strengthen my flabby spiritual muscles, to reverse the direction of my gaze, to make me eager to look at You only.

"I know You want a resurrection thrust inside me and an end to my doubts and negative thinking. In the wake of this will come new life and health. If not on this earth, then I will go into the next life with the differentness that You want for me."

Then Jesus led me to the sixteenth chapter of John where I was stopped by this magnificent verse:

> . . . it is profitable—good, expedient, advantageous—for you that I go away. Because if I do not go away, the Comforter (Counselor, Helper, Advocate, Intercessor, Strengthener, Standby) will not come to you—into close fellowship with you. . . .
>
> John 16:7 AMPLIFIED

These are the blessed functions of the Holy Spirit promised by Jesus:

> *Counselor* (He gives wisdom to the simple.)
> *Helper* (He lifts us over every obstacle.)
> *Advocate* (He is our personal lawyer to "take us on" and plead our case.)
> *Intercessor* (He stands before the throne of grace.)
> *Strengthener* (He gives us vitality and courage.)
> *Standby* (He is always at our side.)

How can a one of us get along without any of those things!

Then glorious verse 33 (italic added):

> I have told you these things so that *in Me* you may have perfect peace and confidence. In the world you have tribulation and trials and distress and frustration; but be of good cheer—take courage, be confident, certain, undaunted—for I have overcome the world. —I have deprived it of power to harm, have conquered it [for you].

11

Resurrection

*T*hanks to Pastor Robert Bonham and the ministry of other loving friends and family, Catherine made good progress during September, October, and November 1982. To my amazement she decided we should accept the invitation to fly to Cape Cod to spend Thanksgiving with her son Peter, his wife, Edith, and their three children, Mary Elizabeth, thirteen, Peter Jonathan, nine, and David Christopher, two. Mother Wood, ninety-one, insisted she would go too.

There were moments of hilarity en route. Since Catherine and her mother both needed wheelchairs to traverse airport terminals, I took over when porters were not available, jockeying both wheelchairs through gates and up and down ramps.

It was Catherine's first visit to the Marshalls' new home, a joyous

*family time with four generations interacting, sometimes peacefully,
sometimes through tensions that bubbled with creativity.*

*At Christmastime, our own home was the scene of another family
reunion. Chet and his wife, Susan, arrived with our new grandson,
Jacob LeSourd, joined by Linda and Phil Lader and our younger son,
Jeff. Christmas had been a time when the perfectionist in Catherine
ran her ragged with holiday preparations. Now for the first time in
twenty-three years, Catherine let others run the show and simply
enjoyed herself. Gift-giving and elaborate meals had been reduced,
allowing more time for games and family talk.*

*At the beginning of 1983 Catherine set several goals for herself.
An 800-page draft of the novel had been completed, but needed months
of work to sharpen characterization.*

She wanted to resume writing for each issue of The Intercessors
newsletter.

And do an article about her mother for a Guideposts *series on
aging.*

*At the end of January, however, she underwent a cataract opera-
tion. From her journal:*

February 9th . . . I am staggering under what the eye surgeon said
to me yesterday during a routine checkup following the cataract surgery: "You are sick from head to toe." I did not have to accept this
verdict, but I did. Now I really have to ditch it—with the Spirit's help
and by God's grace. This verse has truly helped me:

> And if the Spirit of Him Who raised up Jesus from the dead dwells
> in you, [then] He Who raised up Christ Jesus from the dead will
> also restore to life your mortal (short-lived, perishable) bodies
> through His Spirit Who dwells in you.
>
> ROMANS 8:11 AMPLIFIED

February 24th . . . Have hit a new low. I am quite out of breath—
indeed, gasping for air—just in walking from room to room. My
doctor could find no obvious cause for the trouble yesterday. Today it
hit me. . . . Once again the doctors neither know what is wrong, nor
how to help me. So . . . I am backed up against Jesus' help.

March 9th . . . In my Quiet Time, this thought: my hospital experience of the crucifixion was centered on the matter of breathing. This morning the Holy Spirit reminded me once again: "Jesus took your breathing problem into His own body on the Cross so that from henceforth *He* is your life-breath."

With great heaviness of spirit I drove Catherine to Bethesda Memorial Hospital on March 11th, where she was admitted for more tests. We made light of it. "Just a few days," I assured her.

Silently, however, I was recalling another hospital episode almost twelve years before. A daughter, Amy Catherine, had been born to Peter and Edith Marshall and been given her grandmother's name. The baby, however, was genetically damaged in lungs, kidneys, and brain. Doctors at Children's Hospital in Boston offered no hope.

Friends from around the country gathered to pray for little Amy's healing. God answered the prayers, but not the way we expected. Healings occurred . . . in the people who came to pray. Amy Catherine died.

Catherine was desolate for months. "What went wrong?" she wept.

Eventually, she saw it—nothing went wrong! God is a sovereign God. We can plead with Him, bargain with Him, rail at Him, and claim anything and everything in His name. In return God overwhelms us with His blessings, but retains the decisions about "times and seasons" in His hands.

Here is Catherine's last journal entry made in the hospital:

March 12th . . . The blood test yesterday showed carbon dioxide level in my blood too high, but not dangerous; not enough oxygen in the blood, however. Another problem seems to be anemia.

This morning Jesus told me once again: "Keep your eyes off yourself and look steadily at Me. I love you. I know how to mend you."

That very day Catherine was taken to the same Intensive Care Unit where she had spent so many weeks last summer, and put on a respirator. Shortly after midnight on March 18, Catherine's heart

*stopped beating. The Lord had come to take her with Him to experience
the joyous resurrection she missed last summer.*

In the hours and days that followed, the Lord seemed to place all of
us in the family under His special love and protection; plus a necessary
degree of numbness. The calls, letters, cards, flowers, and food that
flowed in warmed and nourished us.

Two triumphant occasions followed: the burial service in National
Presbyterian Church, Washington, D.C., conducted by its pastor and
Catherine's close friend, Dr. Louis Evans, Jr., with her son, Peter John
Marshall.

And the memorial service at the New Covenant Presbyterian Church,
Pompano Beach, Florida. Pastors George Callahan along with Dr.
William Earnhart (church elder and Catherine's personal physician)
shared their memories of a great lady.

Robert Bonham, the man who for so many hours ministered healing
to Catherine as pastor and friend, spoke these words at this same
service:

"During Catherine's funeral in the National Presbyterian Church,
my eyes went to some beautiful stained glass windows through which
the sun was shining. I thought of Jesus telling His disciples, 'You are
the light of the world.' Catherine as a 20th century follower put her
light on a lamp stand so that all might see.

"I looked at the glass in those windows and thought about all the
pieces therein. There were dark pieces and light pieces, all kinds of
colors blended together. I thought about the suffering experiences that
Catherine had early in her life and recently in the hospital. These were
deep, deep colors. Her body never was able to keep up with her mind
and her spirit. It always hauled her back.

"There were, of course, the brighter colors, the rose tints of love and
warmth—the giving of her heart to those in her family and to everyone
she touched. Those colors went out across the United States and
throughout the world. I remember years back when I was at the

University of Illinois, one of the professors there had a hydrocephalic child. He told me that he had called Catherine up long distance and had asked her to pray for his child. She did and the child was healed. All the way to Illinois, and other places far and near, went those pieces of radiating light—warm, bright, healing colors falling on the lives of people.

"There were so many pieces in her life—the books that she and the Lord wrote—the articles for *Guideposts* and other magazines. She wrote nothing that did not have all of her heart and mind in it as well as the heart and mind of Christ. Starting *The Intercessors* not long ago, she and Leonard mobilized prayer warriors across the nation to bring help to many people. Her family represents warm, glowing pieces of glass in the mosaic of her life. Likewise her many friends who kept calling when she died and could not believe that this had happened.

"A surprising thing about a stained glass window is that when the light is not shining through, it comes across as dull. Have you ever looked at a stained glass window when there is no light behind it? You cannot see what is in it. Catherine always had Christ's light shining through her life. As the light of Jesus radiated through the stained glass mosaic of her life, all of us who were within sight of it got blessed.

"When the sun goes down, the horizon stays bright for a long time. There is going to be a long afterglow to Catherine Marshall LeSourd's life. The books that were written will go on to become classics in Christian literature. The articles will go on helping people. There are things she has written that will yet find their way into print to bless us. Her touches on our lives will live on, ministering to my children, and my children's children.

"In the last page of her book *To Live Again*, Catherine wrote these words as she faced life without her husband, Peter: 'At moments when the future is completely obscured, can any one of us afford to go to meet our tomorrows with dragging feet? God had been in the past, then He would be in the future, too. Always He had brought adventure, high hopes, unexpected friends, new ventures that broke old patterns. Then in my future must lie more goodness, more mercy, more adventures, more friends. Across the hills, light was breaking through the storm clouds. Suddenly, just ahead of the car an incandescent, iridescent rainbow appeared, hung there shimmering. I hadn't seen a rainbow for a long time.' And then Catherine's last sentence, 'I drove steadily into the light.'

"Catherine is doing that right now—moving steadily into the Light."

Catherine's Scriptural Lifeline _

*E*arly in her marriage to Len, Catherine formed the habit of copying into a gray 10 by 7 inch notebook the Bible verses that helped most in health or household crises. Over the years the pages filled to become a kind of scriptural lifeline. In the summer of 1982, when she was in the Intensive Care Unit, too ill to read the handwritten entries herself, a member of her family or close friend would read them to her. Here are 41 verses[1] to which she clung with ever-growing assurance:

> Behold, I am the Lord, the God of all flesh; is there anything too hard for Me?
>
> Jeremiah 32:27
>
> The grass withers, the flower fades, but the word of our God will stand for ever.
>
> Isaiah 40:8
>
> He has bestowed on us His precious and exceedingly great promises, so that through them you may escape (by flight) from the moral decay (rottenness and corruption) that is in the world because of covetousness (lust and greed), and become sharers (partakers) of the divine nature.
>
> 2 Peter 1:4
>
> God is faithful—reliable, trustworthy and [therefore] ever true to His promise, and He can be depended on; by Him you were called into companionship and participation with His Son, Jesus Christ our Lord.
>
> 1 Corinthians 1:9
>
> So shall my word be that goeth forth out of my mouth: it shall not

---

[1] All passages from the Amplified Bible unless otherwise noted.

return unto me void, but it shall accomplish that which I please, and it shall prosper in the thing whereto I sent it.

Isaiah 55:11 KJV

And if the Spirit of Him Who raised up Jesus from the dead dwells in you, [then] He Who raised up Christ Jesus from the dead will also restore to life your mortal (short-lived, perishable) bodies through His Spirit Who dwells in you.

Romans 8:11

So too the (Holy) Spirit comes to our aid and bears us up in our weakness; for we do not know what prayer to offer nor how to offer it worthily as we ought, but the Spirit Himself goes to meet our supplication and pleads in our behalf with unspeakable yearnings and groanings too deep for utterance.

Romans 8:26

And we know that all things work together for good to them that love God, to them who are the called according to his purpose.

Romans 8:28 KJV

I know that whatsoever God doeth, it shall be for ever: nothing can be put to it, nor anything taken from it: and God doeth it, that men should fear before him.

Ecclesiastes 3:14 KJV

For the Lord is our judge, the Lord is our law-giver, the Lord is our king; He will save us.

Isaiah 33:22

For I, the Lord your God, hold your right hand; I, Who say to you, Fear not, I will help you!

Isaiah 41:13

For God's gifts and His call are irrevocable—He never withdraws them when once they are given, and He does not change His mind about those to whom He gives His grace or to whom He sends His call.

Romans 11:29

When the enemy shall come in like a flood, the Spirit of the Lord will lift up a standard against him and put him to flight—for He will come like a rushing stream which the breath of the Lord drives.

Isaiah 59:19

But God is faithful [to His Word and to His compassionate nature], and He [can be trusted] not to let you be tempted . . . beyond your ability and strength of resistance and power to endure, but with the temptation He will [always] also provide the way out—the means of escape to a landing place—that you may be capable and strong and powerful patiently to bear up under it.

1 Corinthians 10:13

The Lord redeems the life of His servants, and none of those who take refuge and trust in Him shall be condemned or held guilty.

Psalm 34:22

Though I walk in the midst of trouble, You will revive me; You will stretch forth Your hand against the wrath of my enemies, and Your right hand will save me.

Psalm 138:7

The Lord also will be a refuge and a high tower for the oppressed, a refuge and a stronghold in times of trouble [high cost, destitution and desperation].

Psalm 9:9

And He will establish you to the end—keep you steadfast, give you strength, and guarantee your vindication, that is, be your warrant against all accusation or indictment—[so that you will be] guiltless and irreproachable in the day of our Lord Jesus Christ, the Messiah.

1 Corinthians 1:8

He will swallow up death in victory—He will abolish death forever; and the Lord God will wipe away tears from off all faces; and the reproach of His people He will take away from off all the earth; for the Lord has spoken it.

Isaiah 25:8

Fear not; for I am with you; do not . . . be dismayed, for I am your God. I will strengthen and harden you [to difficulties]; yes, I will help you; yes, I will hold you up and retain you with My victorious right hand of rightness and justice.

Isaiah 41:10

I have called you by your name, you are Mine. When you pass through the waters I will be with you, and through the rivers they shall not overwhelm you; when you walk through the fire you shall not be burned . . . nor shall the flame kindle upon you. For I am the Lord your God, the Holy One of Israel, your Savior. . . .

Isaiah 43:1–3

For though the mountains should depart and the hills be shaken or removed, yet My love and kindness shall not depart from you, nor shall My covenant of peace and completeness be removed, says the Lord, Who has compassion on you.

Isaiah 54:10

For thus saith the Lord God, the Holy One of Israel; In returning and rest shall ye be saved; in quietness and in confidence shall be your strength.

Isaiah 30:15 KJV

In the world you have tribulation and trials and distress and frustration; but be of good cheer—take courage, be confident, certain, undaunted—for I have overcome the world. —I have deprived it of power to harm, have conquered it [for you].

John 16:33

I assure you, most solemnly I tell you, the person whose ears are open to My words—who listens to My message—and believes and trusts in and clings to and relies on Him Who sent Me has (possesses now) eternal life. And he does not come into judgment—does not incur sentence of judgment, will not come under condemnation—but he has already passed over out of death into life.

John 5:24

Do not fret or have any anxiety about anything, but in every circumstance and in everything by prayer and petition [definite requests] with thanksgiving continue to make your wants known to God. And God's peace . . . which transcends all understanding, shall garrison and mount guard over your hearts and minds in Christ Jesus.

Philippians 4:6–7

But they that wait upon the Lord shall renew their strength; they shall mount up with wings as eagles; they shall run, and not be weary; and they shall walk, and not faint.

Isaiah 40:31 KJV

Whoever takes a drink of the water that I will give him shall never, no never, be thirsty any more. But the water that I will give him shall become a spring of water welling up (flowing, bubbling) continually within him unto eternal life.

John 4:14

My sheep hear my voice, and I know them, and they follow me: And I give unto them eternal life; and they shall never perish, neither shall any man pluck them out of my hand. My Father, which gave them me, is greater than all; and no man is able to pluck them out of my Father's hand. I and My Father are one.

John 10:27–30 KJV

Keep and protect me, O God, for in You I have found refuge, and in You do I put my trust and hide myself. . . . my body too shall rest and confidently dwell in safety.

Psalm 16:1, 9

In the day when I called, You answered me, and strengthened me with strength (might and inflexibility) [to temptation] in my inner self.

Psalm 138:3

Now the Lord is the Spirit, and where the Spirit of the Lord is, there is liberty—emancipation from bondage, freedom.

2 Corinthians 3:17

(For the weapons of our warfare are not carnal, but mighty through God to the pulling down of strongholds;) Casting down imaginations, and every high thing that exalteth itself against the knowledge of God, and bringing into captivity every thought to the obedience of Christ.

2 Corinthians 10:4–5 KJV

Behold God, my salvation! I will trust and not be afraid, for the Lord God is my strength and song; yes, He has become my salvation. Therefore with joy will you draw water from the wells of salvation.

                                                                    Isaiah 12:2–3

Rejoice in the Lord always—delight, gladden yourselves in Him; again I say, Rejoice!

                                                                    Philippians 4:4

Although the fig tree shall not blossom, neither shall fruit be in the vines; the labour of the olive shall fail, and the fields shall yield no meat; the flock shall be cut off from the fold, and there shall be no herd in the stalls: Yet I will rejoice in the Lord, I will joy in the God of my salvation. The Lord God is my strength, and he will make my feet like hinds' feet, and he will make me to walk upon mine high places.

                                                                    Habakkuk 3:17–19 KJV

Heal me, O Lord, and I shall be healed; save me, and I shall be saved; for You are my praise.

                                                                    Jeremiah 17:14

Thou wilt keep him in perfect peace, whose mind is stayed on thee: because he trusteth in thee.

                                                                    Isaiah 26:3 KJV

Our inner selves wait [earnestly] for the Lord; He is our help and our shield. For in Him does our heart rejoice, because we have trusted (relied on and been confident) in His holy name.

                                                                    Psalm 33:20–21

. . . for He (God) Himself has said, I will not in any way fail you nor give you up nor leave you without support. [I will] not . . . in any degree leave you helpless, nor forsake nor let [you] down [relax My hold on you]. —Assuredly not!

                                                                    Hebrews 13:5

For I am persuaded beyond doubt—am sure—that neither death, nor life, nor angels, nor principalities, nor things impending and threatening, nor things to come, nor powers, Nor height, nor depth, nor anything else in all creation will be able to separate us from the love of God which is in Christ Jesus our Lord.

Romans 8:38–39